# THE VOICES OF AIDS

Also by Michael Thomas Ford

# 100 Questions & Answers about AIDS
What You Need to Know Now

# THE VOICES

## OF AIDS

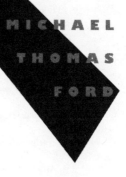

TWELVE
UNFORGETTABLE
PEOPLE TALK
ABOUT HOW AIDS
HAS CHANGED
THEIR LIVES

MICHAEL

THOMAS

FORD

MORROW JUNIOR BOOKS • NEW YORK

Printed in the United States of America.

1  2  3  4  5  6  7  8  9  10

*Library of Congress Cataloging-in-Publication Data*
Ford, Michael Thomas.
The voices of AIDS / Michael Thomas Ford.
p.  cm.
Includes bibliographical references and index.
ISBN 0-688-05322-X
1. AIDS (Disease)—Miscellanea—Juvenile literature.
2. HIV-positive persons—Miscellanea—Juvenile literature.
[1. AIDS (Disease)]   I. Title.   RC607.A26F654 1995
362.1'969792—dc20   95-10629   CIP AC

# Contents

# Acknowledgments

The hardest part of putting this book together was choosing from among the many people who have stories to tell about how AIDS has affected their lives. I was fortunate enough to speak with dozens of people who took time to share their experiences with me, and I regret that I can include only a handful of their voices here.

I also owe much to the women and men at AIDS organizations across the country who offered suggestions, provided contacts, and patiently answered my many questions, and to Jeffrey Naiditch, M.D., for checking the medical facts. Thanks also to my editor, Andrea Curley, who made it all come together, and to Kathryn Hinds, who, as always, knows how to say it all a little bit better.

I would especially like to thank my friend Regina Sackrider, former Speakers' Bureau coordinator at the National Association of People with AIDS, for her help with this project and the last one, for her laughter, and for having the cutest cats in Washington, D.C.

# Introduction

Do you know anyone with AIDS?

If you're like most people, you would answer no to that question. But if you don't already know someone with AIDS, the chances are that someday you will. In fact, you probably already do and just don't know it. AIDS could be affecting the person who delivers your mail, the person who sits next to you in class, or the person who coaches your soccer team. A person with AIDS could be the singer you see on MTV, the actor in your favorite film, or the anchorperson on your evening news program.

There are millions of people in the United States alone who are living with HIV, the virus believed to cause AIDS. Yet unless one of them tells you, you would probably never know that she or he is infected. While many people believe that those infected with HIV are all thin and sick-looking, most people living with HIV and AIDS look as healthy as everyone else does. And for every woman, child, and man living with the effects of HIV or AIDS, there are dozens of uninfected people who are somehow affected by that person's illness. They are the friends, parents, lovers, brothers, and sisters of people living with AIDS.

*The Voices of AIDS* contains the stories of twelve people whose lives have been changed by this illness. Some of these people are infected with HIV; some of them are not. Some may be just like you. Others may be very different. But even if they have nothing in common with you, I hope that you will listen to what they have to say. Their stories are meant to show you how AIDS has touched every kind of person imaginable, from a family in Missouri to a teenage AIDS activist in New York City, from a man who uses pop music to provide AIDS information to a woman who cares for children with AIDS. You will also hear some of the many stories of women and men infected with HIV who live happy, healthy lives, including the friend who inspired me to write this book and a young woman who went to an AIDS organization for help and is now its director.

All of the people in this book have stories to tell, and all of them have something to say about how AIDS is changing the lives of individuals from all walks of life. When you read their stories, remember that they are the people who live around you. You might see them in the grocery store, at the beach, or in church. When you read or hear about AIDS, remember their stories. Someday you might find yourself in their place when someone close to you tells you that he or she has AIDS.

Throughout this book you will also find a number of AIDS Fast Facts. These will give you some basic information about AIDS, including how it is and isn't transmitted, how you can protect yourself from becoming infected, what you can do to fight AIDS, and some of the common misconceptions concerning it. There is also a list of places that you can write to or call for more information. I hope that you will read this information and use what you learn to educate others. Together, we can all work to encourage understanding of this frightening disease and the growing number of people who live with it every day of their lives.

—*Michael Thomas Ford*

# What Are HIV and AIDS?

In this book, the two words that you will see most often are *HIV* and *AIDS*. In order to understand AIDS, it is important to know what HIV and AIDS are and how they differ from each other. Unfortunately, this can be very confusing, because people tend to use them incorrectly to mean the same thing.

The difference between HIV and AIDS is actually very simple: AIDS is a condition, and HIV is the virus that most scientists believe causes that condition. Because HIV is believed to cause AIDS, it is also sometimes referred to as the AIDS virus.

First let's examine **HIV**. HIV stands for *human immunodeficiency virus*. This is a long name, so let's look at each word separately. A *virus* is a microscopic organism that causes a disease. When you have the flu, it is because you were exposed to a flu virus that somehow got into your body. HIV is a virus that causes a disease.

The word *human* indicates that this virus affects only people, not animals. HIV is a virus that causes a disease in humans.

The impressive-sounding word *immunodeficiency* refers to the immune system, the system of the body that fights off infections. When you are exposed to a virus, it is your immune system that protects you from getting sick by attacking and destroying the virus. If the immune system has a deficiency, this means that it is not working as well as it should and that the body is no longer able to effectively fight off the viruses that cause infection.

Put all of this together and you see that HIV, the human immunodeficiency virus, is a virus that damages a person's immune system so that it is not able to fight off infections as it should.

Now, let's talk about **AIDS.** Like *HIV,* the word *AIDS* is the short version of another long term, *acquired immunodeficiency syndrome,* or *acquired immune deficiency syndrome.* Again, if we look at each word separately, it becomes easy to understand what AIDS is.

Saying that AIDS is *acquired* means that it is something you must get from someone else; it is not something that you inherit from your parents, like black hair or green eyes. You have to get it from someone who already has it.

As you now know from the definition of HIV, *immunodeficiency* means a condition in which the immune system is not working properly.

A *syndrome* is simply a group of symptoms that indicate that there is something wrong.

AIDS is therefore an acquired condition in which a person's immune system has stopped working properly. To be more specific, AIDS is a condition in which a person has been infected by the human immunodeficiency virus (HIV) and has developed certain infections because her or his immune system has been destroyed by HIV to the point where it is no longer able to fight off the infections.

When a person has been infected with HIV, we say that he or she is HIV-positive. But just because a person has HIV does not mean that this individual has AIDS. It's only when the person's state of immunodeficiency reaches a point where the person develops certain infections, cancers, or tumors or has very low numbers of specialized cells to fight off infection that we say that the individual has AIDS. A person can be HIV-positive for many years before developing AIDS, which is why it is important to understand the difference between HIV and AIDS. When we say that someone "got AIDS" from someone else, we really mean that he or she got HIV, which may develop into AIDS at some later point.

*Gabriel Morales*

# COMING OUT PROUD

*When nineteen-year-old Gabriel Morales speaks to young people about living with HIV, he speaks from personal experience. At seventeen, when he was a junior in high school, he tested positive for the AIDS virus. Today Gabriel is a peer educator in San Francisco, where he tells other young people about the effect HIV has had on his life. He is also attending college, where he is studying psychology and anthropology.*

**How did you find out that you are positive?**
I went to an anonymous test site to get tested. I actually planned my test around my spring break, because I was going to Palm Springs with my friends. It was a big event for me, and I decided that I wanted to get tested before I left. When I went to get my results, they were inconclusive. So they had to do the test again, and I went away on vacation not knowing

4

whether or not I was positive. When I came back, I found out I was positive.

**Why did you get tested?**
I knew that teenagers should get tested. I had tested before, when I was sixteen, and I had been negative. But I knew in the back of my mind that there was some reason that I had the idea to get tested again. I wasn't having safer sex. I had gotten the educational message about condoms, but my low self-esteem made it impossible for me to tell someone who was ten to twenty years older than myself that he should be using condoms when he had sex with me. It wasn't that I didn't have the education, it was that I just didn't know how to use it to my advantage.

**How did your parents react?**
I haven't told them yet. I am moving out of the house soon, and I plan on telling them then. My father and I don't really have a close relationship, so it's really my mother I'm worried about. Ever since I came out to her about being gay, everything has been so much better between us, and I've gotten closer to her. So it will be really hard to tell her this. She knows where I'm working, and what I do and all of that. But I just haven't been able to disclose to her that I am HIV-positive.

**Do you think she has any idea?**

I think she does have an idea. But it's the same as with the issue of my being gay. She had the idea that I might be, but she denied it because she wasn't able to accept it until I actually came out and told her I am gay. I think it's the same with HIV.

**What do you think her reaction will be?**
My mother knows a lot of my friends who are HIV-positive. But it will be much harder when it's her son she's dealing with. I know she's going to cry a lot. I think she will be shocked, and will think that there is something that she can do to save me by sheltering me and spoiling me. I made the decision when I was seventeen to wait until I was out of the house to tell her because of the way she is. She's a big part of my life; she knows everything about me except for this. She's very overprotective. This will be a lesson for me, because I will have to educate her about a lot of things.

My father I don't know about. I hope it's an eye-opener for him. He comes from a very upper-class family, and for them everything can be solved by doing something or buying something. And that's part of why I'm where I am now. I grew up thinking that nothing would ever affect me because I was surrounded by this bubble and protected by them. They think that everything happens to everybody else and that it will never happen to them. So that's one of the things that I hope for my whole family, that they will come to see that they are not out of reach of things like this. I want to tell them early on in my illness so that they can become educated before I am sick with AIDS and dying. I want to be able to work through our family problems before it's too late.

**Aren't there times when you want to share with them?**
Yes, now more than ever. When I had just a regular job working at a bank, it was easy to keep my home life and my AIDS life separate. I would go to my speaking engagements and my support group and that would be my release. Now it's a lot harder, because I work in the AIDS field every single day and I've gotten so accustomed to talking about HIV and AIDS. When I say that I'm HIV-positive, it's no big deal to me anymore, unless I'm telling someone who doesn't know me. I joke around about it so much that it's become easy to say it.

Sometimes I'll be talking at home, and I have to catch myself before I accidentally say something. That's really hard. It reinforces for me the negative way people look at this disease. It also brings back all of the negative feelings I've ever had about being gay. Because I know my family will think that this would never have happened to me if I weren't gay. Even though I know that's not true, it's hard not to relive those feelings.

**Is that why you don't tell them?**
I think it has a lot to do with it. But I've been able to accept both my HIV and my gayness to a point where I know that I'm not HIV-positive because I'm gay. I'm HIV-positive because I had so little education about being able to empower myself and protect myself. I thought that it was something that happened just to older gay white men and IV drug users. I didn't think it was going to happen to me, because I was young and was going to live forever.

The invincibility issue is the biggest thing that affects teenagers. That and the fact that teenagers are obviously going to take risks. It's a time in your life when you are forming your own identity, and no matter what anyone tells you, you are going to take risks until you learn for yourself. And unfortunately, with AIDS, once you make that mistake, it's too late.

**What was it like to learn that you're positive at such a young age?**
I had a crash course in HIV. I didn't know there was a difference between HIV and AIDS. I thought that having HIV would give me AIDS the next day and I'd lose all of this weight overnight. I thought that I would die really soon. It was really hard, because I had to cut school in order to go get my results, and when I got back to school they told me I had to serve a couple hours of detention. My first thought was, I don't have that many hours left. But sitting in deten-

tion, I had all of this time to read, and I read about HIV and learned what it all meant.

## Did you go to a support group?

When I first found out about a support group for young people, I was all excited because I thought there would be people there my age, all teenagers. But when I got there, everyone was in their twenties and I was the youngest one. The first night, I just sat and listened, and that helped because I saw how people had been living with HIV. But I still felt like they weren't my age. When you're seventeen, people who are twenty-two seem so much older to you.

## Did you tell any of your friends?

I told some of the people I worked with at my job in a supermarket. There was one girl in particular that I was close to. One night we were at her house talking, and she noticed that my facial expression had changed in response to something that she'd said. So I told her, and she was very supportive. Then she told me that her father had died of AIDS, and just learning that helped me. All of my friends responded well, and I really admire them for that. It's a lot easier for me to be with them because I can still hang out with them and feel like one of them; and because I know that they are all HIV-negative, it's a release from HIV for me. I don't have to think about it when I'm with them.

**How did your gay friends react?**
I only told one of my gay friends. He was someone that I had met when I was fifteen, a sophomore in high school, and had been dating on and off. I told him I wanted to get tested, and he got tested as well. His results came back negative, so when he found out that mine were positive, he was shocked. He came over and talked to me. He was very supportive.

**We were talking earlier about the fact that you found it hard, as a young man, to ask older men you were sleeping with to use condoms. Is that a common experience for young gay men?**
I think it is. It creates a dynamic where you have a person who is older than you, and after having older people tell you for years what to do, you find it hard to tell this older man what to do and how to do it. And if you've never had any education about your sexuality, and no one has ever told you that being gay is fine, it's a lot harder.

When you go to bars at an age younger than you should, which is how many young gay men try to meet other people, you are naturally going to get picked up by men older than you are. And for me, that was validating in a way, because I felt like there was somebody who found me attractive. I was very centered around my looks, because I thought that it was all about how you looked and that you were important only if people found you attractive enough to sleep with.

So there you are with this man who is older than you are, and it's hard to tell a person older than you what he should be doing. We've always been told that you shouldn't talk back to your elders or disrespect them. And when it comes to a situation where you're in bed with someone, you don't want to be rejected by that person, especially if having sex with him is your only way of feeling like you're a real person and feeling validated.

**Did any of your partners ever suggest using condoms?**
One or two did, but most of them assumed that because I was young I wasn't infected.

**A lot of people would say that because there is so much information out there about HIV and AIDS that young gay men should be able to protect themselves better.**
Those people don't see the whole picture. All we ever hear about is how wonderful gay life was back in the 1970s and how sex was free and everything was about freedom. As a young gay person, you feel like you're missing out on what older men had back then. And even though HIV is a danger now, many young people feel like they are missing out, so they ignore that risk. There's also that belief that

you can tell who has it and who doesn't.

It's really all about trying to fit in. I don't think that older gay people have any right telling younger gay people that if we are infected it's somehow our fault. We still grew up having no identity, and we still grew up with self-esteem issues. And that makes us powerless. And, in many cases, we are having sex with older men. So they should take the initiative and teach us about safer sex. That's what it comes down to. Because most of the teenagers I know have sex with older men. And someone had to infect us. It wasn't like it just popped into our bodies out of thin air.

**So if providing information about HIV and AIDS isn't enough, how do we reach young gay men?**
It has to start by changing the way that gay people are perceived. Last night I was flipping through the journal that I kept from 1989 to 1991. I was fourteen years old. And I was crying while I was reading what I'd written. I couldn't even write the word *gay* back then. I would write that "this person is that way, just like me" or "I can't believe people are actually happy being that way." If I had been taught at an early age that being gay was a positive thing, and that it was just a normal, healthy way of living, that would have been so helpful. Throughout this whole journal, I always wrote "that way" instead of "gay." And there is so much of my life that I never even wrote down

because I was afraid somebody might find the journal and read about it. I really wish that someone had told me that the thoughts and feelings that I was having were fine, that it was perfectly fine to be gay.

**As a young gay man, do you feel as though AIDS has cheated you?**
The thing I think I've been cheated of is my childhood, my adolescent years. I had to develop an identity in about a week, not in the years that most young people get. I had to develop an understanding of what was happening to me and what was going to become of me. I couldn't think like a teenager anymore. I had to think as a teenager who was developing along with living with HIV.

As a gay man, I feel like I've been cheated of a lot of things. Because even in the gay community there is still a lot of ignorance about HIV and a lot of prejudice against dating someone with HIV. A lot of people are scared and don't really understand what it's like to live with HIV. There's still a lot of fear, and there's a lot of guilt in regard to being negative or positive. I was cheated of being able to grow up gay and negative and not having to think about a time line, just to be somewhat carefree as a young person just growing up. I never had the chance to live with the freedom of accepting myself as a gay person, because right after I started to come to terms with my sexuality and be happy, I found out I was positive.

**Did you feel like you would never be able to have sex again?**

I thought that I would never have sex again because no one would ever want to have sex with me. Now I don't worry about it. My self-esteem is wonderful now, and I feel like I am a great person. Now when I meet people and start dating them, I have certain expectations of what should happen in the relationship. When those things aren't there, I end it. I am in no rush to be in a relationship, because I see all the work involved in it.

I realized a while ago that by having sex randomly I was giving so much of myself to people that they didn't really deserve. I thought that by having sex I was getting the validation that I was attractive and worth something. Now I know that I don't have to do that to be worth something. I am a great person, and I don't need anyone else to tell me that.

**Did being HIV-positive change the way you had sex?**

At first I didn't tell my partners, because I hadn't even fully dealt with it yet. I did start taking the initiative to have safer sex, though, because I felt that if I could have prevented myself from being infected by practicing safer sex, then I could prevent my partners from being infected.

It's not until now that I've felt able to discuss my HIV status with potential partners. When I do decide to be in a relationship, I will tell the person I'm with. If he can't handle my being HIV-positive, then it's not a relationship I want to be in. HIV is a big part of my life, so he has to take that along with me.

Everybody should assume that everyone else is positive. Because then we all would be taking precautions and nobody would get infected. As it is now, everyone assumes everyone else is negative, and that's why people get infected.

**How did you come to the point where your self-esteem rose?**
I think it was just the friendships I formed. Growing up, I never had friends. I was always a loner. I wanted to have friends, but I could never relate to people. Then I came to realize that I am a really great person to be friends with. When I look at myself now and think about what has happened to me, I can't understand why I let it happen or why I let people do what they did to me to make me have no self-esteem. I'm happy now just being myself and not being fake, not trying to project an image that isn't me—just gaining acceptance of myself. I'm so much happier now, and I feel like I can be who I am and be who I want to be.

**Do you think you would have reached this point if you hadn't tested positive?**
I don't know. I was reading in my journal this thing I wrote about going to meet this guy I had met over the

phone. I was writing down what I was going to wear, and I kept writing about how good I would look. It was like someone else was giving me positive reinforcements about my looks, but it was me writing them down. Now I look back on what I wrote, and I know I didn't really feel that way. And I can't believe I was like that, trying to convince myself how great I was because I was actually so scared.

**How has your life changed the most in the last two years?**
I have doctors' appointments that I never had before. I have to give so much blood that I never had to give before. I have to watch what I eat. I have to make sure that I'm taking care of myself. The thing that's changed the most is really all of the doctors' appointments. I never went to the doctor before. Now I go all the time and have to give blood. I remember in high school that I would have to leave school early to go to the doctor. I would sit in his office and wonder how many other teenagers had to do the same thing. It made me feel so alone.

**How did you go if your parents didn't know?**
I had insurance through my parents. But because I didn't want them to know, I couldn't use it. Luckily, San Francisco provides health services for young people with HIV. But I was lucky. If you don't have insurance, you can't do anything. I was so afraid of

going because I thought they would tell my parents. And I also didn't want bills coming to the house, because my mother opened all the mail, and I knew she would see them.

**Do you have days when you get really angry about being positive?**
I do. It's not anger around myself, though; it's anger around seeing people get sick and seeing nothing being done about it. I get really angry when I see another person who is really young get infected because the system has gone wrong. Because so many people try to put the blame on that young person, but it's not that person's fault at all. There were certain things that person obviously didn't know that caused him to become infected, skills he was never given to protect himself. So I get angry at the system, not at myself or at anyone else. I get angry that there is so much work to be done that people aren't doing.

**What do you think the biggest problems are?**
I see a lot of heterosexual women of color and young gay men coming in who have recently been infected. These are groups that we still aren't reaching, and we aren't talking about their issues.

**Why don't we talk about those issues?**
I think, especially for communities where people are infected through sex or drug use, they aren't talked

about because those things are not talked about in our society. Sex doesn't happen, unless it's between married people. Sex is something that isn't clean and isn't fun. And drug use is so looked down on that it just reinforces the blame that people feel and keeps them from talking about their problems with drugs.

I think it all comes down to people letting people be. Letting go of all of our hang-ups and letting people live without asking them to explain why they do the things they do. We also have to let people feel free to talk about what's on their minds.

The biggest issues are the invincibility issue and self-esteem issues. And thinking that AIDS is a gay disease is still a big issue with young people. So many heterosexual young people come in and say they never thought they would be at risk because only gay people got it.

And for young people who are gay, there are other issues. If you are in denial about your sexuality, you won't admit that you're gay, even if you are having sex with people of the same sex. When I wrote in my journal that I was "that way," I didn't think that I was gay. I was having sex with men, but I wasn't gay. And that allowed me to think that I wasn't at risk, because I wasn't really gay. A lot of young men who are having sex with other men think that way, because it's easier than dealing with all of the issues that come up once you acknowledge that you are gay.

**What do young people need to know most?**
By putting a face to HIV, we are showing young people that it can and will happen to some of them. It will continue to happen unless people sit down and think about what they are doing. I'm speaking from a biased viewpoint because I have really worked on my self-esteem and I feel able to bring up these issues. A lot of young people don't feel strong enough to do that, or to bring up the issue of using condoms. The teenage years are such a crucial time because you feel that you want to grow apart from everything that you've ever been taught. And at the same time there are usually some feelings of low self-esteem. So it's hard to tell young people to be assertive about safer sex or about caring for themselves when they probably don't have very high opinions of themselves. But that is what needs to happen.

# How Does HIV Cause AIDS?

While it is not important to know every scientific fact about HIV and AIDS, it will help you to understand how AIDS develops if you know a little about how HIV works.

There are many parts that make up your immune system and allow you to fight off infections. One of the most important parts is a group of cells called *T4-lymphocytes.* Commonly called T-cells, they are a type of white blood cell. There are a great many of them inside your body, between six hundred and fifteen hundred per cubic millimeter of blood. This is good, because they fiercely protect you against any invading virus by telling other cells, called *killer lymphocytes,* to attack and destroy the virus before it can reproduce and make you sick.

Scientists aren't sure why, but T-cells cannot deal with the AIDS virus effectively. HIV is able to alter its structure so that T-cells don't recognize it and therefore don't tell the killer lymphocytes to attack and kill it. By the time the T-cells recognize it, the virus changes again, so the T-cells have to start all over to fight it. The situation is like trying to coach a football game against a team that keeps changing the rules every time your team is about to make a touchdown.

But that's not the only thing HIV does. HIV is able to enter T-cells and live inside them. Then it does something really tricky. The cells in your body reproduce by a complicated process called *transcription,* in which they read the genetic code they are made up of and then make a perfect copy of themselves, almost like running a picture through a copy machine. But HIV is able to fool the cell it is hiding in and convince it to make a copy not of itself, but of the AIDS virus. HIV then destroys the cell it is living in and moves on to another one. It repeats the same process over and over again until the immune system is swarming with copies of the AIDS virus.

In the meantime, the T-cells are being destroyed and aren't producing any copies of themselves to replace the dying cells. As more and more of the T-cells die, the infected person's T-cell count (the number of cells per square millimeter of blood) drops. When this happens, the infected person's immune system is no longer able to fight off infections, and he or she can more easily develop any number of infections, diseases, and cancers. When a person's T-cell count drops to two hundred or below, or when that individual develops certain infections because his or her immune system is failing, then that person is said to have developed AIDS.

But just because a person is said to have AIDS, she or he is not necessarily sick. Some people infected with HIV have lived for several years with T-cell counts of less than twenty! Other people have very high T-cell counts but get sick anyway, because HIV spreads from their immune system to other parts of the body, such as the nervous system. But in general, the lower a person's T-cell count, the more likely she or he is to get sick, and a person's T-cell count is a pretty good indicator of how well his or her immune system is doing in fighting the AIDS virus.

*Eileen Mitzman*

# A MOTHER'S VOICE

*In March 1989, Eileen Mitzman's daughter Marni, then twenty-four, developed a persistent case of pneumonia. After several tests failed to identify the cause of Marni's illness, her doctor suggested that it was related to HIV infection. Marni called her former boyfriend, whom she had been involved with for several years when she was in her late teens, and asked him to be tested for HIV. He was positive. Slightly over two years later, in July 1991, Marni Mitzman died of AIDS-related causes.*

*Shortly after her daughter's death, Eileen became involved in Mothers' Voices, a group made up of parents who have either lost children to AIDS, have children with HIV, or are simply concerned about the number of people living with the disease. One of the most successful AIDS activist groups operating today, Mothers' Voices*

*was the first AIDS organization to be invited to
the White House to speak with President Bill
Clinton.*

*In a speech written shortly before her death,
Marni wrote a message to other young people
who, like herself, believed they would never be
affected by AIDS:*

*"I'm a strong, independent fighter. I was
always proud of that. Now, at twenty-six, I
moved back home with my parents so that they
can take care of me when I am too weak to get
out of bed. I lost a lot of friends, and it's hard to
meet new people because you have to explain
about your illness. Even then, you notice that
people treat you differently. People who try to be
nice don't realize I don't want any special treatment, just understanding. The only way to have
understanding is through knowledge. Learn
about HIV, AIDS, and testing. Don't think,
'Well, just this one time.' In 'just this one time'
you can get AIDS. I never spoke to people before;
I'm usually shy. I did this today for my sister and
parents and for you. I was sitting there with you
nine years ago—now I have AIDS. How many of
you are going to say that? It's up to you."*

*Marni never got to give her speech, but today
her mother carries her daughter's message to anyone who will listen.*

**How did you get involved in Mothers' Voices?**
When Marni died, my husband and I got involved with a group called Community Research Initiative. One day two young women—Ivy Duneier and Lily Rundback—came in to tell us about their idea, called Mothers' Voices. They felt that there was a need for the families of people with AIDS and families of people who had died of AIDS to speak out and to lobby the government for research, for care, for prevention, and for education—for the government to come out and make a bigger deal out of the crisis than it was making. A much bigger deal.

So we started with a small group of mothers, and we now have hundreds of thousands of mothers across the country who simply lobby their local government and their local house of representatives, so that they in turn bring the issues to Washington, to their senators and congresspeople. We have found that there are families sitting all over the world all by themselves with no one to talk to. And this group has given them an opportunity to come out and speak up and speak out. It's empowering—it's very empowering. You don't feel helpless and hopeless. You feel like you can make a difference. And we are making a difference.

**What are some of the things Mothers' Voices does?**
The first major thing that we did was go to Houston, to the 1992 Republican convention, and meet with

everyone who was there who would talk to us. We went onto the floor of the convention and we spoke mother to mother. And that's completely different from speaking politically. There is not a mother who would send a child to war. And if mothers ran the world, there would never be wars. So now, with AIDS, mothers have become like lions protecting their children.

**How did Marni's illness affect your involvement in Mothers' Voices?**
Marni was already gone when I got involved with Mothers' Voices. But from the time that we discovered that Marni had become infected, I knew that I had to make a difference, and I had to do something to save her life. And I had to do it really fast. So I read and learned as much as I could so that I could become a research scientist, a doctor, an educator, a caretaker, a caregiver—all of those things. And I really did a hell of a job. But I lost the battle. And I don't intend to lose the war. I'm now in this war for everyone else's child, because there is a great deal at stake here.

I had been in a mothers' support group while Marni was HIV-positive and I enlisted some of those people for Mothers' Voices. And we continued to grow and grow into a larger and larger circle of people. People were coming out of the woodwork with stories. Some were not public, because either they didn't want to be or their children didn't want them to be. In the groups, you were able to speak to one another.

So I urged the mothers to get out there and fight, and they felt better and better about their situations because they were not sitting and wringing their hands and pounding their chests anymore. And I was not going to do that. That was the part of the support group that I didn't enjoy. I did not want to be a victim. I wanted to be able to make something happen. And we are making it happen. We have wonderful meetings with congresspeople, senators, and their aides. We met with the president. And we've learned a great deal. We know a great deal.

And everyone will listen to us, because we are moms. Everyone has a mom, and we are not just moms whose children are infected, but moms who are afraid that their children are very much at risk. Because of that, we will eventually list as our members every single mother in the world. Because everyone has a mom. And whole families get involved— sisters, brothers, fathers, cousins, aunts, uncles. It's really quite an extraordinary idea.

**What was your first personal experience as an activist?**
The first time that I spoke out about our story. It was at a meeting in the home of someone who was going to organize a fund-raising luncheon for Mothers'

Voices so that we could start out with some money to
go to Washington and get other mothers to join us
there. And this very young woman, who had three
young children who were just fine, stood up. She had
decided that her children were at risk, just as she
had been at risk growing up in the 1980s. She had
escaped AIDS, and she felt that this was an opportunity for her to do something for people who hadn't or
people who might still be at risk. Then they asked me
to get up and speak and tell my story. It was the first
time I had ever spoken publicly, and it was quite a
thing for me.

The first time I was an activist in the traditional
sense was at the Republican convention in Houston.
Mothers' Voices had marched earlier at the Dem-
ocratic convention here in New York—were very
much a part of it, as a matter of fact. But Houston
really made me feel good. I was going to where
they needed to be converted, not where they were
already converted. And I was just amazed at how
many women we spoke to, more than were in
our own group, who said, "Thank God you are
doing something; the Republican party has really
failed us with this disease." And then more and more
women came out and confided to us, saying, "I have
a son, I have a nephew, I have a brother, I have a
cousin." All infected. But nobody knew, because
these people were scattered all over the country and
this was a disease that was not being talked about. So

they were very happy to hear us out there talking about it.

Of course, there were some who backed away from us like we were going to give them AIDS. But that was not the rule; that was the exception. So, we got the feeling that people were looking at us like, here they are, here are the mothers. They were also scared about what could happen to their children, or what had already happened to their children.

**Did the success of that convention encourage you to do more activism?**
After that, we continued to mobilize and continued to keep speaking to the powers that be in our government. We must have the government. We realize that the private sector cannot possibly raise enough money for this disease, because it is an epidemic. It is a plague, actually. So we keep saying to the members of Congress, "How come there is money available immediately when there is an earthquake, when there's a flood, when there's a hurricane, but there's no money for AIDS?" The money is there; we know it's there. And this disease is much worse, because our children are losing their lives. It's like a war. We need a commander in chief, just as the country has in a time of war. There must be someone in charge. And why the politicians aren't treating the AIDS epidemic that way is the thing that frustrates us and motivates us at the same time.

We go to Washington with these pictures [pointing to a shelf of photos of her friends and daughters]. Each one of us carries a framed picture of our children, of our families. We put these down on their desks and we say, "Look at these children. They look just like your children in the pictures on your desk. And we are going to help you save your children from this dreaded disease."

**What is the response of the politicians you meet with?**
Well, they keep telling us—the ones who are sympathetic—that they understand and that they are working on it. And some are. Some are working very hard. But for the most part, they tell us that there is no money, and we just don't want to hear that. So then we tell them that there's money for everything else; why is there no money for this? But they are lumping AIDS with other diseases. And we are trying to unlump it from other diseases.

I went to see Senator Stevens from Alaska on one of my first visits to Washington. And he told me that there is no problem with AIDS in Alaska. And I said, "Well, there will be. If there isn't right now, then there will be." I said, "My daughter lost her life to AIDS at the age of twenty-six. Not her house to a hurricane or an earthquake, but her life." And he said, "Well, we have people in Alaska who are dying of cancer." And my response was, "At twenty-six, Senator?" And he walked out of the room. Now, I'm sure I made my point. He was telling us that the private sector had to take care of AIDS. And we were telling him otherwise. You have to keep hammering away at these people. I'm sure that something of what I said stayed in this man's mind.

**What did Mothers' Voices say to President Clinton?**
We asked for his help. We told him that we must have his help. That he has to be in charge of this, and that we need a much more important person and people working for him in the AIDS world. I don't think that the president has given this thing the attention that it deserves.

**Do you think that Clinton understands?**
I do think he understands. But I'm not sure about what he's doing. Because when he came in and made gays in the military his first priority, my first thought was, "First they have to live before they can go into the military and get killed for the government." That was ridiculous. I didn't understand how that could be a priority for him.

**Did you ever think AIDS would affect you?**
No. They said it was a gay disease and that if gay men stopped having sex with one another, the disease would go away. Or if IV drug users stopped using dirty needles, they would stop getting it. So it didn't

really sound like a very serious thing, at least not the way the government was presenting it.

In 1989, when my husband called me to tell me that they thought Marni had AIDS, I said, "Don't be ridiculous; girls don't get AIDS." Now, I was not a person who had my head buried in the sand. But they weren't telling us then that there was something going on. They knew what was happening with this disease; they just didn't tell us.

I never dreamed of the scope of this. And it's shocking to me now, because almost every single day I get a phone call from someone who has just found out that someone close to them has AIDS. I am now part of a network that people call for information, for help, for support. They call to become involved. We have mothers in just about every state in the U.S.

**That seems to be part of your power, that you are not as concerned with being an organization as you are with supporting one another.**
We are mobilizing the hearts and voices of the mothers of this country. Which to me is the most important thing you can do, to get people to speak up and speak out and let everyone know that this is not acceptable. We cannot turn to our children, whoever are left of them in the next generation, and say that we just stood by while this decimated their generation.

**There's a whole group of children now who have to live in fear of loving someone else.**
Exactly. Black or white, gay or straight, young or old. It's affected everyone. Everyone is at risk. It's a horrible, horrible disease. And what's so horrible about it is that just because you love somebody and want to sleep with somebody, you are at risk of getting this disease. One of the greatest pleasures of humankind is now deadly. This is crazy. This disease is crazy.

**What emotions drive parents when they see their child struggling with HIV?**
My emotion was to save my daughter's life. I had to save her life. It was my responsibility, and therefore I had no time for anything else. My attitude was, we are going to cure this disease. We are going to get the correct medicines until we find a cure. And we are going to save her life. And we need the government, and we need the doctors, and we need the researchers, and we need everyone to know what is going on so that everyone can help us. I just wanted to enlist everyone.

We were public five seconds after we knew about Marni's illness, because it was of utmost importance to us that people knew that a twenty-four-year-old girl was sitting in the hospital with a disease that they were telling us was only a gay and drug users' disease. Well then, how was this possible? I wanted to find out if there were more of us out there. And if there were,

I wanted to mobilize as quickly as possible and let the world know so that we could start to protect it immediately and at the same time start to cure it.

**In 1989, when Marni was diagnosed, there was still very little information about HIV in women. What was it like not being able to get any information?**
It was very frustrating. You have two choices: You can sit and wring your hands in frustration or you can get out and fight. People can do either thing with anything that happens in their lives.

**Is that what is most important for parents in that situation to realize, that there are places to get information?**
Yes, especially for parents in rural areas. People in larger cities don't have that problem so much anymore. I felt very alone being the mother of a daughter with AIDS as opposed to being the mother of a gay man at that point, because no one believed women got it. I wasn't differentiating, but the thing that suddenly struck me was, "Oh my God, there are a lot of girls out there who are at risk and don't know it. Let's tell them. Let's not just sit and wait for Marni to die. Let's try to save her life and their lives."

**How did it affect Marni, watching you fight for her so hard?**
I don't know. It's very hard to put yourself in the place

of someone who's diagnosed as having a life-threatening disease. And I always talked about it as nothing other than that: life-threatening. I was as optimistic as possible because I believed it. I was sincere. It was not something that I was pretending to be for her sake. I really thought that we could overcome this, because people do fight and overcome life-threatening diseases. And there are many long-term survivors with AIDS who are alive from the beginning of this epidemic to today. There are things we still don't know about it, but we are learning more and more every day.

**What are you proudest of in your involvement with Mothers' Voices?**
We have gotten mothers from all over the country involved in making a difference. We have empowered mothers and families to feel that they have a voice and that they can speak out and be heard. We have mobilized a great many people who were sitting by themselves. And we have done some great education seminars as well, and perhaps have saved a lot of lives that we will never know about. That's a very good feeling, to know that you can get the message out that our children are at risk and that we have to make sure that they are educated.

**What is your message to parents afraid to talk to their children about AIDS?**

They must not assume that their children are not having sex, because there is a very good chance that they are. And if you think that they are going to listen to the message that they should abstain, then you are a very foolish parent. It's like not telling them that if they walk out into the street they could get hit by a car. I think it's every parent's obligation to talk about AIDS. It used to be that the worst that could happen when you had sex was a woman could become pregnant before she was married. But there was nothing like this then.

**Does AIDS consume your life?**
Yes, a great deal of the time, because I think it's a very important issue. And the reason I talk is because I am always trying to convert people, saying, "Listen to me: It could save your children. Listen to me: We can get rid of this disease. Help us. Join us. Be part of us."

It's not a twenty-four-hour-a-day thing. I go to the movies. I go to dinner. I talk with friends. But usually somewhere in there is conversation about AIDS. Because there is a message here. And I tell people, "I'm not doing this for my child. I can't save my child, because she's already gone. I'm really doing it for yours and everybody else's." I'm not a person who is a zealot. I am a mother. A mother without children who doesn't want other mothers to lose theirs.

One of the most important things for people to understand is that they should never doubt that a small group of thoughtful, committed citizens can change the world. Indeed, it's the only thing that ever has. And we really believe that. We really believe that we can and will make a difference. And without us, there is nothing. Without everyone speaking up and fighting, it won't happen.

# AIDS FAST FACT NUMBER
## *Three*

## How You Get It

In order for you to become infected with HIV, you have to be exposed to someone else who already has the virus. But unlike such other viruses as cold or flu viruses, which can be transmitted through the air—when someone sneezes—or orally—by drinking from the same glass as someone who has the virus—HIV can be transmitted only when your bloodstream comes into contact with the *body fluids* of someone infected with HIV.

The body fluids that carry HIV are blood, semen, vaginal fluids, and breast milk. Semen is the sticky fluid that is secreted from a man's penis when he ejaculates. Vaginal fluids are the liquids secreted inside a woman's vagina. Breast milk is the milk secreted by a woman's breasts, usually after pregnancy.

Even though these fluids can contain HIV, just touching them or getting them on your skin is not enough to infect you with HIV. The virus must come into contact with your bloodstream. This can happen in four ways:

• sharing an infected needle to inject drugs or steroids

• through any sexual activity where another person's body fluids come into contact with open cuts on your mouth, vagina, penis, or rectum

• getting a blood transfusion with infected blood

• by an infected mother passing it along to her unborn or nursing child

Other related ways the virus may be passed from one person to another are just variations of these main means of transmission, such as:

• rubbing open cuts on your body together with those of someone who is HIV-positive in blood-brother or blood-sister oaths. In this case, the infected person's blood is being put into direct contact with your bloodstream, in much the same way as when you get a transfusion.

• piercing your body or getting a tattoo with an infected needle that has been used on someone else and not cleaned properly, which is just like injecting drugs or steroids with a dirty needle

Basically, that's it. And since the AIDS crisis began, all donated blood is now tested for the presence of HIV, so there's almost no chance of your becoming infected through a transfusion. That means you really only have to worry about being infected in two ways—through unprotected sexual activity and through sharing needles to inject drugs or steroids. And if you know how to protect yourself in these situations, you know how to protect yourself against AIDS.

*Kyle Craney*

# A BROTHER'S STORY

*Kyle Craney is what many people would call a typical all-American boy. At seventeen, he is the president of the senior class at his Missouri high school. He sings in the choir, practices tae kwon do, and plays basketball and soccer. He describes his family as middle-class, churchgoing Christians, much like many of the families in the Midwest, where he lives. And like many people, he never thought that AIDS would touch his life. But when Kyle was fourteen, he found out that his sister, Carrie, is HIV-positive.*

*Four years earlier, when Carrie was twenty, she had given blood at a church blood drive. Following Red Cross procedure, the blood had been tested for HIV and found to be positive. Carrie had been infected by her long-term boyfriend, whom she had been planning on marrying.*

*Since then, both Kyle and Carrie have spoken to people all across the United States about what it is like to live with HIV and what it is like to have a loved one discover that she or he has the virus. This is Kyle's story.*

**What was it like to find out that Carrie was HIV-positive?**
I was very scared. I didn't know what to do. I just didn't understand it at all. I'd heard about AIDS because of the Magic Johnson case, and that helped because it made me understand that HIV was not just something that happened to people who did the wrong things. It was frightening, but I didn't understand why I was frightened. I could look at Carrie, and she looked perfectly fine from my viewpoint. She didn't look sick. She didn't even look pale. She looked perfectly normal. So I couldn't understand how she could have this virus inside of her.

Plus, I had lived with Carrie all of my life. All of a sudden, I'm told that she has had a time limit put on her, that there is now this limit on how long she might live. All this time, I had no idea she had the virus. Then they tell me my sister won't live but another five or ten years. And that's real hard to take.

**Did they tell you she might die?**
At the time she was diagnosed, they told her she might have only a year at the most. Then at other

times they told her she might have only a few weeks, especially when she was sick. Now there is no time limit. It's just whenever things start going wrong. But seven years ago, they thought she would just go downhill and die.

## Did Carrie know about HIV and AIDS when she found out?

She didn't even know what AIDS was. They told her she had it, and she was like, "What's AIDS?" She had no idea what HIV was. No one did. There was no education then, no word about it. When she found out, they called her on the phone and told her she might have the virus. They told her not to tell anyone. The only ones who knew were Carrie and my parents. No one else knew, not even her doctors. She only went to doctors provided by the Red Cross.

## Did she tell her boyfriend?

She told him, and he was tested, and of course was HIV-positive. But he is in complete denial about it. As far as I know, he never even contacted a doctor. I think he still thinks that this can't be happening to him. She stayed with him for a long time after they found out—almost five years—partly, I guess, because both of them felt that no one else would want them. They loved each other, and they wanted to be together. But it just didn't work out.

**Were you angry at her?**
No, I wasn't angry at her at all. I never felt that it was her fault that she got it. It just happened. There was no reason for me to be upset with her, because she had been faithful in her relationship. It was her boyfriend who wasn't.

**Were you angry at him?**
I didn't know the details about what happened to her until a year or so after I found out that she had HIV. I never really questioned it. I just accepted that she was HIV-positive. And I had no reason to suspect him, because I had known him for a long time and always thought he was a great guy. I had no idea it would turn out this way, or that it would turn out to be because of him. I never really blamed anyone; I was just upset that she had it. I was just trying to deal with the fact that my sister, who had almost been my mom in many ways, was now going to die and that she couldn't have kids or a family of her own.

**Had you had any exposure to information about AIDS before this?**
The only information I received was whatever I'd gotten at school, but I can't remember ever getting any. Otherwise, everything I knew was because of Magic Johnson. I had no idea it would ever affect my family. Because everyone said it was a gay disease or a disease for people who deserved it. Now here we are, a

middle-class family living in a town we've lived in all our lives, and my sister has it. She was in college. She was in a relationship for more than four years, and they were planning on getting married and having kids. That's what they were looking forward to. Then she finds out this, and it's kind of a slap in the face because she was planning on having the rest of her life and suddenly she finds out she can't have it.

**Did you feel you had to keep it a secret?**
I found out a few days before my family told our entire church congregation, so I didn't really feel like I had to keep quiet about it. The church gave us total support, which we never expected. It was strange, because I had heard that someone was coming to speak to our church about AIDS, but I had no idea who it could be. Then I found out it was my sister. Then there were all of my friends, and I didn't tell them who this speaker was going to be, because I wanted it to be a surprise. They were all talking about it ahead of time, and I wanted to hear what they had to say.

**How did it go—telling your church?**
Usually there were about fifty people in church, but this night there were like five hundred. They were all listening. They had all grown up with Carrie, and, looking at her, they couldn't see what was wrong with her. So it hit them all really hard, because they never

thought that it would happen to anyone that they knew.

**Were there any bad reactions?**
No, there really weren't. No one has ever said anything negative to her. The only thing that I can think of is one time when she spoke and a girl put a tissue in front of her face because she was afraid she could catch the virus by Carrie breathing on her. But that's why Carrie speaks, because she wants these people to realize that they are actually more of a threat to her than she is to them. Because she can catch whatever they might have and not be able to fight it off.

**Did you have any bad reactions at school?**
People ask me how she is, but nobody ever says anything. This year I will be the student-body president of my high school, and I'm very well known at school. So people will ask me questions, but nobody says anything bad. When Carrie came and spoke to my school, it hit a lot of people very hard. A lot of people cried at the assembly, and a lot of people came up to her afterward to thank her. And a lot of people stopped participating in the risky behaviors they were involved in when they heard her speak.

**How did you educate yourself about AIDS?**
Carrie educated me. I didn't know anything about AIDS, nothing at all. She would go over what it was

about, what it was, and all of that. I had no idea I was going to have to deal with all of this. It was the summertime, right before my first year of high school, and I thought I'd have all summer to hang out. Then all of a sudden I was told my sister is HIV-positive, and suddenly I wasn't sure that I wanted to go to high school, because that was where she had gone and everyone would know her. I wasn't embarrassed, but I was shocked. I felt that people might look at me differently, and I was afraid of that. I didn't want to be the one that they went around and talked about. So there were times when I worried about that, but I realized that I had to be there for her and I had to start dealing with it all.

**Were you ever afraid you might get it from her?**
I questioned it. But I realized pretty quickly that if I was going to get it from her, I would already have gotten it. She had moved back home and had been living with us for two or three years already before I found out. I remember one day I went upstairs and asked her what would happen if I drank out of a cup she had used. Then I thought about it and realized that I'd been sharing drinking glasses with her and eating off of the same plates as her for years.

Another thing is that at first I thought that if my sister had it, then I wanted to have it too. Because if she was going to go through it, I wanted to go through it with her.

**Do you forget that she has AIDS?**
When I'm with her now, I really forget about it. Because if you spend your whole life with someone, and she's the one who always baby-sat you and was the one you always talked to, then you really don't have a chance to look at her and see her differently. She doesn't look any different just because now she has this virus inside her. If she had lost an arm or a leg, then I could see that she was different. But when I look at her, she's exactly the same person. She's a little tired sometimes, but I don't see the problems inside, and it's easy to forget that something's wrong inside her. Then suddenly she has to go into the hospital for some reason, and it really hits me hard that she's sick.

**When did you start speaking publicly about AIDS?**
The first time I spoke was right before I found out Carrie was coming to speak at my high school. I spoke with her at a very tiny school outside of our town. You have to understand, I didn't have any speaking experience at all. I'd never spoken in front of a crowd. It was just all of these things coming together, and I just felt that it was the right thing to do. So I spoke with Carrie at that school, and I was very nervous. But after that it got easier. Now I speak whenever I can. It's hard, though, because I'm still in school and I don't have the time to speak as much as I'd like to.

**Why did you start speaking?**
I was speaking because I felt people needed to know what Carrie was going through, and also what it was like for me. Also, I wanted to be by her side when she spoke, to support her. I didn't want her going through it alone. Besides, she was speaking in places where people knew me, like my school. I wanted people to feel comfortable coming up to me and asking me questions if they wanted to. I thought that if they saw me speaking, then they would see me as someone they could approach with questions.

**What do people want to know most?**
They want to know what they can do to not get HIV. They don't want to hear about abstinence or about not doing things that they might be doing. They want to know what they can get away with and still be safe.

I think the problem is the fact that young people still don't understand that it doesn't matter what you look like or how you think or how you act. They think that if they're good-looking or they are doing good things or are healthy, for some reason they won't get infected. They don't understand that the virus wants to get inside the body. It won't grow on the outside. So they look at other people and at themselves and they look at the outside. They think that if the outside is healthy-looking, the inside must be as well. And that's why it gets passed so easily. If you

perform any of the acts that can result in the transmission of HIV, you can get it.

**Do we do enough education?**
Yes, I think we do. It's just that you're dealing with
teenagers, and with teenagers everything goes in one
ear and out the other. I know it does with me a lot of
the time. And this crisis is really going to hit teenagers
the hardest, because those are the years when you
start experimenting with sex. It's already killing a generation.

We did this demonstration once where we gave
glasses of water to thirty kids in a classroom. Then
everyone shared their glass with two or three people.
Then we put a drop of dye into each glass, because a
substance had been put into a few of the glasses, and
the dye would show which glasses now had the substance after being passed around from person to person. And twenty-eight out of the thirty glasses had it.
And that's what the AIDS virus is like. If you sleep
with someone, it's like sleeping with everyone that
person has ever slept with and all of the people those
people have slept with and on and on. And young
people don't get it. They think that a condom will
protect them from everything, but condoms don't
always work.

**Do you think we should teach teenagers to "just say
no"?**

That's not realistic. There's just no way teenagers are going to just stop. We've seen that over and over again. You just cannot preach abstinence over and over. Teenagers are normal human beings, and they are going to forget sometimes. Kids have hormones, and people have to realize that hormones are not going to go away just because suddenly there's AIDS to worry about.

If people are going to have sex, then they have to be told about having safer sex. But they also have to realize that safer sex doesn't make the virus go away. They are still taking a chance. They think that it's okay because it's love, and there isn't supposed to be any danger involved with love. So when you think you're in love, it seems so great and so beautiful, and you can't imagine that anything bad will come out of it.

**How does it feel knowing that people your age and younger are growing up in an age when loving someone else could be deadly?**
It's really hard, because love is supposed to be really special. But the fact is that you just can't tell when someone you're going to be with is telling the truth. I learned that from my sister's experience. And that makes me very angry, because it makes love something you have to be afraid of. I look back on these movies that show how teenage love used to be, so free and easy, and it's sad. Nowadays you walk down the

street and feel like there's this danger everywhere.

There's so much pressure put on teenagers now that I think a lot of them just don't care about anything. There's a lot of drinking and drug use as a result of this pressure, and that makes young people care even less. They just want to escape, because it's too hard to think about living with the threat of all of these things.

**Do you feel that AIDS takes away a lot of your choices?**
It does for people like myself, who have seen what AIDS can do. But I think that most people still don't consider the fact that someday they might be dealing with it. Magic Johnson showed the world that anyone could get it, but I know that still didn't change me too much until my sister got it. It's not going to change everyone at one instant.

Sex makes you feel good, and when something makes you feel good, it's hard to imagine that there's anything wrong or dangerous about it. It's sad, because love and sex are something that two people share with each other. And all of a sudden, something that is supposed to be so great is so deadly, and nobody understands that, because there doesn't seem to be anything harmful being done when it's being performed. In love there is supposed to be nothing harmful. With drugs, it's easy to see how it could be harmful to you. But with love, it seems so beautiful that you can't imagine it being deadly. It's really destroyed romance.

What's sad is that you just don't know who you can trust. You could go out with someone for years and years and think you know everything about that person. But that person could be infected and not even know it, or could know but be afraid to tell you out of fear of losing you. With AIDS, you might not even know you have the virus. You could get drunk or high one night and maybe have sex with someone. You might not even remember doing it. Then you can go for years with this virus inside you and not even know about it until you get sick. During that time, you could infect twenty or thirty other people without even knowing it.

If there was some outward sign that would show who had the virus and who didn't, this crisis would be over by now. But there are no outward signs until the last stages of the disease, and that's why it keeps going and going and going.

**How has the AIDS crisis affected you the most?**
I know I wouldn't be on student council or be a national AIDS educator if it weren't for AIDS. It's changed my perspective on life—seeing how short it can be. It's made me, my family, and my friends more aware of what can happen. I question a lot of things that I never did. But then again, if there aren't things in life to question, then it's not much worth living.

**Has it made you make decisions you wouldn't have had to?**
My life is totally different now. I never took life that seriously until this happened to Carrie. Now I try to make everything I do make a difference in some way. It brought me out to show that I'm here to help. Before this, I never volunteered or did anything like that. Now I'm the student-body president, and I'll be involved in all of these different things.

**What have you learned most about people?**
I've learned that no matter what you tell people, a lot of them aren't going to listen to you, and there's not much you can do about that. But I also understand that if you give people a chance and a choice, they can make big changes in their lives for the better. I've learned to listen to people, and that has helped me out tremendously. I've also learned to deal with life one day at a time.

I've seen lots of different sides of the world because of AIDS, in that I've been around a lot of different kinds of people, people that others might think are bad or wrong for whatever reason. But they're all human beings. They just have different feelings. And I don't understand why we can't just look at people as people.

**What do you think of people who say that AIDS is God's punishment?**

They just need to learn a little more about life and what it's all about. They need to get closer to God. But there are always going to be people like that, and you just don't listen to them. That's how they feel, and they have to be willing to change and see different points of view. This is not God's punishment on anybody.

I still deal with that in some ways. I still don't understand why God let this happen to Carrie, why he put this on her shoulders. She's educated a lot of people, and made a difference in a lot of people's lives, but it still doesn't seem fair that she has AIDS. And at the same time, it's been put on me, too. I understand that God doesn't put things on you that you can't handle. But I still know it will be hard when anything happens to her.

There's a lot of questions I have, and there are still things I don't understand. Carrie was always the kind of person who stayed out of trouble. She didn't go out and party or anything. Then all of a sudden she is told that she has AIDS. I did wonder why it happened to her and not the guy down the street who was doing drugs and having women over all the time. So there are questions you have, and they are hard to answer.

**What's the hardest thing to deal with?**
The thing that's hardest is watching people die. My sister had a very close friend who died. In the last six

months before he died, there would be times when he didn't know who he was or who she was. He went blind. He couldn't hear anything. He would go crazy. And my sister saw all of this. And I think that's something that really hurt me, to realize that someday I could walk into my sister's room and she could see me and I could see her but she might not know who I am. She'll look at me and just not know me. I hope that never happens, but there is always the possibility that it will.

**Do you talk about that?**
We have on occasion. I don't like thinking or talking about death. She knows what's going to happen, but I'd rather not discuss it, because it makes us both upset. It's good that we do talk about it once in a while, but it's something that I don't like bringing up and my parents won't bring up. Maybe it would make it easier if we did talk about it more. But there's no going back with AIDS. It's going to happen no matter what, and however it happens, it happens. I don't know how talking about it would make watching it any easier. I'll talk with my mom about it, but not with my sister. I don't want her feeling guilty or getting sick because she worries about it.

# AIDS FAST FACT NUMBER
## *Four*

## How You Don't Get It

Because HIV must reach your bloodstream directly in order to infect you, HIV is different from viruses that can be contracted through casual contact like shaking hands or kissing. Some of the ways you *can't* get HIV are:

- kissing someone with HIV

- sharing silverware or drinking glasses with someone with HIV

- using the same toilet as someone with HIV

- performing mouth-to-mouth resuscitation or other lifesaving procedures for someone with HIV

- living in the same house or going to school with someone with HIV

• being sneezed or coughed on by someone with HIV

• shaking hands or hugging someone with HIV

• playing sports with someone with HIV

• swimming in a pool with someone with HIV

• getting spit on by someone with HIV

• from your dentist. While there have been some cases where people have claimed to have been infected by their dentists, these claims have not been proven and may be false. In any event, almost all dentists now wear gloves, which protect their hands from any blood in your mouth and your mouth from any cuts they might have on their hands. They also follow strict sterilization guidelines for cleaning their instruments after each use, which means that you cannot be infected with HIV if your dentist has used a tool on an HIV-positive person and then uses it on you.

In other words, you can't get AIDS just by being around people who have it unless you have sex with them or share needles with them! While the list of things you can't do with people with HIV or AIDS is very short, the list of things you can do with or around people with HIV or AIDS is endless. Don't let fear stand in your way. Educate yourself and get the facts.

## Dini von Mueffling

# LETTING LOVE HEAL

*Alison Gertz had it all. She was a member of New York's social elite, and her world of money and parties seemed completely removed from the reach of AIDS. She was young, beautiful, and happy. She had a steady boyfriend, and everyone thought she had a promising future ahead of her. Then, in 1988, she found out that she was HIV-positive. She had been infected during a single sexual encounter with a man she had met one night at a club.*

*After learning of her infection, Ali decided to take her story public, and became one of the first young women to openly discuss living with HIV. As a speaker, she taught many people that, when it comes to being at risk for HIV infection, it doesn't matter who you are, how much money you have, or where you live. She made many people aware that the AIDS crisis was touching many more lives than was ever believed possible, and shortly before her death in 1992, her story was made into a television movie starring Molly Ringwald.*

*Unfortunately, Ali's story is not an uncommon one. Once mistakenly believed to be at low risk for contracting the AIDS virus, women who become infected through sexual contact are now the fastest-growing group of people being devastated by the AIDS epidemic. In many areas, AIDS is the number-one killer of women. Yet there are still very few studies of the effects of HIV in women.*

*Dini von Mueffling was one of Alison Gertz's best friends. Watching her friend live with and die from AIDS, Dini became one of the millions of people who, although not infected themselves, have had their lives touched by the AIDS crisis. Today, Dini and Ali's friends Stefani Greenfield and Victoria Leacock continue to tell Ali's story and spread her message through Love Heals, an AIDS education organization that reaches thousands of young people each year.*

**Tell me about the way Love Heals was formed.**
It was Ali who started Love Heals. When she was first diagnosed, in 1988, she decided that she wanted to do something. She thought what she wanted was to start a foundation that gave help to people with

AIDS. So she created Love Heals. Then when she became public, she became overwhelmed with the role of being a public person, and Love Heals fell by the wayside. In 1992, when she was quite sick and we knew that she was dying, some of us decided that we wanted to do something special for her and thought that maybe what we should do was resurrect Love Heals.

Ali died in August of 1992, and we opened our doors in November. What we wanted to do was continue her work, and we decided that we would be an educational organization. There were a lot of organizations out there doing what she had wanted to do four years earlier, when she was diagnosed, which was helping people with AIDS. But there weren't any foundations that I was aware of focusing primarily on prevention and education for young people, which was what Ali had been doing with the last three years of her life. So that's what we decided we would do, to keep her message going.

**What is the focus of Love Heals?**
The idea behind Love Heals is the education of young people by young people. And although we might not be as young as we were a few years ago when we started all of this, that's really our philosophy—that young people respond to other young people educating them, particularly when those other young people know what they're talking about.

Initially it was just the three of us going into schools. We would show a short video about Ali, and then we would talk about what it's like to have your best friend go through this. Now we also do a lot of education in terms of facts and understanding how you can get AIDS and how you can avoid getting it. We don't talk about just the physical issues, but also the psychological ones. We talk about being with somebody and negotiating safer sex and having a positive self-image.

**Does that approach work well?**
It works great. We've reached over fifteen thousand kids directly in less than two years. We've traveled all over the country. And I hope we've saved some lives.

**Is this something you ever thought that you would be doing?**
Not in a million years.

**How did you feel when Alison told you she had AIDS?**
Actually, somebody else told me, because she was so sick. The shock was incredible, particularly because this was in 1988, and in 1988 women were not being diagnosed with HIV and AIDS as a result of heterosexual sex, let alone through one single sexual encounter.

**Did you have many moments of wondering how you were going to deal with her illness?**

I had many, many moments of asking myself that. When someone you know is diagnosed as being HIV-positive, first of all you have to educate yourself. And for me, I had to understand what it meant for me as her friend. Even though I knew how you could and couldn't get it, there were still people who were telling me not to get too close to her because we didn't know everything about the disease. And that was very hard, to have your best friend going through something like that and other people around you telling you to be careful about being near her. And all along, there were times, when Ali was quite sick and hospitalized, that we had to have discussions that I never thought I'd have to have with her. One conversation we had was me asking her what she wanted me to do in case she died. And this was a year or more before she actually did die. And I felt like she handled it much better than I did. You just don't think you'll ever be talking to your best friend about her death, not when both of you are still in your twenties.

**Did that experience change you?**

A lot of people don't understand this, but AIDS eliminates a lot of the bullshit from your life. It eliminates everything that you don't need, everything that's extraneous. It makes it crystal clear what is really important. Even if you don't have the virus yourself and are just around people who do. It has definitely changed the way I live.

**In what way?**
I'm much more focused than I used to be, from the big things to the little things. The big things being relationships and ending them when I realized that they weren't going where I wanted them to or when I saw that I was hanging on to someone just for the sake of being with somebody.

One of the funny things that has happened was that during the four years that Ali was sick, there were different people that I was dating. But I wouldn't tell her about all of them, because she wasn't able to experience all of the things that I was experiencing, and I didn't think it was fair to tell her. Then I met the man who is now my husband, and we moved in together on our first date. He asked me to marry him three months later. And I freaked. One of the things that I was really worried about was that Ali would think I was abandoning her. And how would I explain to her that I was still her friend and that she could still have me as much as she wanted and needed me? I used to go over to her house for dinner all the time, and we would order in and sit on her bed and eat. And one night I sat down and told her about Richard, and that he had asked me to marry him and I had said yes. Then I waited for her response, and it was, "What took him so long?" It was the most appropriate response, and made me feel so much better. So the next night he came over, and then it was the three of us sitting on her bed eating dinner. And that's what life is all about.

**Were there friends of hers who abandoned her?**
Yes, there were some people who abandoned her. But you know, those people weren't really her friends to start with. If someone can't handle your illness, then they aren't real friends.

**How has being involved with Love Heals changed your life?**
For one thing, I'm not so driven for personal success. I've had to accept a lot of things about how difficult it is to make a nonprofit organization achieve the things you want it to achieve in a world where funding is limited and there are so many other groups fighting for money. It's been really difficult. But the successes are so sweet. There hasn't been a single presentation where a young person, and usually many of them, hasn't come up afterward and thanked us and told us we are doing something wonderful and so important. Often, so many of them have many other questions. So it's very clear that we are fulfilling a need, and it's great to be needed.

**Do you think that we have reached young people enough?**

No, I don't think that we have. This winter we did something called the Clearasil National Teen Summit, where eighty student leaders from every state in the country came together to discuss what they thought the most important issues of their time are. And they picked AIDS. That really surprised the people from Clearasil, who had been hoping that they would pick something like urban violence or racism or something else a little less controversial. And I would say that at least fifty percent of these kids had never, ever had any kind of AIDS education at all. And unfortunately, that's the norm in this country. As a society we have a very difficult time talking about the specific ways that one can get HIV—sexually or through drug use. We have a very difficult time talking about those issues, so consequently we don't talk about them. And that's why teenagers are the second-fastest-growing group of people becoming infected with HIV today, because nobody is telling them these things. And there are so many misconceptions out there. And these misconceptions, I find, have nothing to do with race, class, or anything else. They are just absolutely widespread.

**Do you get any opposition from people who believe that we shouldn't talk about these subjects?**
Sure, especially in the beginning. We had a lot of schools that wanted us to come in, but only if we talked only about abstinence. There was one school

we went into that knew that part of our program is talking about safer sex, but when we got there, they said we could only talk about abstinence, because the person who had arranged the visit was afraid that the principal would get angry. We said we would only do the program if we did the whole program, and we went on. When we got to the safer-sex portion of the program, the lights started mysteriously flickering on and off, and we had to stop.

All the studies that have been done show that, if you go into a school and you talk about prevention, sexual activity rates in that school drop, not rise.

**What do you find young people's biggest fears are?**
I think that their biggest fear is that they feel like they can't talk about the fact that they're afraid of AIDS. They feel like they are supposed to know everything but that they don't.

**What are you most proud of with Love Heals?**
I'm proud that we've directly reached fifteen thousand kids. We've also written some legislation that is currently before Congress. It's called Current Resolution 192, and it came out of some of our frustration with the state of AIDS education in this country. It asks for HIV/AIDS education to be included as part of all health-education classes nationwide. It also asks for the television and motion picture industries to behave more responsibly and respond to the AIDS

crisis by showing safer sex or abstinence as an option and just dealing with the fact that AIDS is a problem. Because right now, the opposite is the rule, and all they show is people hopping into bed and having sex without using condoms. And when there is a show with an issue about condoms, they send out press releases saying, "The guys on such-and-such a show use a condom in Thursday night's episode." They should be doing the opposite. They should be explaining to their viewers why they aren't using them the rest of the time.

Another part of the resolution seeks to encourage condom advertising on television. There is no law against showing condom ads; it's just that networks are afraid to do it. We also asked for the National Commission on AIDS to be reinstated, because it was disbanded in November of 1993 after having made some very valuable recommendations and doing some good studies. We currently have a campaign urging people to write in to their congresspeople and ask them to vote for the resolution.

We also have an amazing project that, if we are able to raise the funding for it, will revolutionize AIDS education for young people. And that is a hot line that we want to establish that kids can call and receive prerecorded information about AIDS, delivered to them by celebrities. The information will be as detailed and accurate as possible, and as current as it can be. The celebrities who sign on have to agree to deliver the right message, in the way that we write it. For example, if they are going to talk about prevention, then they have to talk about all of the different options, not just one or two. Kids from all over the country were asked to pick their favorite celebrities, and that's who we've asked to do it. This hot line will encourage kids to hop from menu option to menu option so that they can get a lot of different kinds of information and not be embarrassed about talking to a live person.

**It's amazing that all of this came out of a friendship.** Friendship and frustration. Immense frustration. This all came out of feeling frustrated. It's great to see that Ali's work can continue, because that's what she would have wanted.

# Risky Business

The riskiest thing you can do when it comes to AIDS is to think that you are not at risk for contracting HIV. Grandmothers, lawyers, quarterbacks, farmers, children, and models have all been infected with HIV. HIV can be found in big cities and small towns, in people who have had sex once and in those who have had sex many times. You don't need any special qualifications to have HIV—you just need to participate in risky behavior.

As long as you believe that there's no way you can get HIV—because you are too good a person, too young, too popular, too smart, or too anything else—you are participating in risky behavior. The world is filled with HIV-positive women and men who never thought that they could end up with the virus. And unfortunately, it takes only one exposure to HIV to become infected. That's one instance of unprotected sex or one shared needle.

Also remember that drinking alcohol or using drugs like pot, ecstasy, or acid can be just as dangerous as injecting drugs or having unsafe sex. Why? Because when you are high on alcohol or drugs, no matter what they are, your inhibitions are lowered and your judgment is not as sharp as it should be. That makes it a lot easier to engage in unsafe sex or in other unsafe behavior. When you're high or drunk, you often feel invincible, and you might decide that a moment of pleasure is worth the risk. It might be fun, but you just might end up paying for it with your life.

*Faye Zealand*

# THE LITTLEST SOLDIERS

*To listen to Faye Zealand tell the stories of the
many children who have come in and out of her
life is to hear the smallest voices of the AIDS
crisis. Since 1985 Faye, a former Head Start
teacher, and her husband, Terry, the former principal of a school for emotionally disturbed adolescents, have been the driving force behind
the AIDS Resource Foundation for Children.
Created to address the needs of children affected
by the AIDS crisis, the foundation offers many
different types of support services to children
and families dealing with the effects of living
with HIV. Its three residential houses offer
temporary homes to children living with HIV
and to children orphaned by AIDS until foster
families can be found to take them in. In
addition, the foundation provides support and
counseling to families dealing with the pres-*

*sures that come from living with HIV on a day-to-day basis.*

**How did you get involved in the AIDS crisis?**
We lost a dear friend to AIDS, and we decided that we wanted to do something to fight this disease. When he was dying, we promised him that we would do this. After his death, we gathered some friends together to discuss what we could do, and the suggestion was made that we talk to people in the AIDS field and find out what the needs were. What we discovered was that there were many, many children out there being affected by the AIDS crisis and that few resources were available. In 1987 we opened Saint Clare's Home for Children. We envisioned it as a home for children with AIDS. With the first child we ever took in, the parents had died of AIDS and no relatives could be located to take the child in.

**Before these programs existed, what happened to children with HIV?**
They were boarded in hospitals. And that's what my husband and I found so alarming. We would go to visit our friend who was hospitalized and we would see these children running around who looked as healthy as our own three children. When we asked why they were there, the doctors said that the children's parents had died of AIDS and either their families could not be found or their families would not

take them in, so they were being housed in the hospital.

Often, the children were there simply because the parent that was still alive could not single-handedly care for the child. There was one father who came every day after work to care for his son, and he never believed that he could ever find anyone who could help him care for his child. Unfortunately, that was a very accurate observation on his part. There was just nothing available. And we still, to my amazement, find that often these children are simply left in hospitals.

**Why were there no foster care programs for these children and their families?**
The foster care system is and always has been heavily overburdened. When suddenly all of these children who had HIV were added to the system, it was more than the system could handle. We felt that foster parents could be found for children with HIV; it was just a matter of people needing to see what we were seeing and needing to know what we knew about the AIDS crisis and how it was affecting children.

In addition to finding foster care situations, we also offer short-term respite services to families who are dealing with the effects of HIV. We see that as a very valuable service, and we often find that it makes the difference for parents. Some parents have been able to go into drug treatment while we've kept their

children. Some foster parents have been able to continue being foster parents because we offer respite
care. Our whole belief is that you can't just give foster
parents a check and give them a child and send them
on their way. We have to continue to be there and
continue to support them if that placement is going
to be successful. And we are delighted whenever we
are able to do that.

**Do you know how many children are infected with
AIDS in this country?**
I try very hard to avoid statistics at all costs, because
they never show the whole picture. The good news as
far as AIDS is concerned is that we're finding out that
in two-thirds or more of the cases where a child tests
positive for HIV at birth, the child goes on to convert
to a negative status by the age of two as the antibod-
ies inherited from the mother leave the body. So the
number of children identified at birth as being HIV-
positive is not an accurate count of the number of
young people living with HIV.

The other thing that has to be considered when
talking about the effect of the AIDS crisis on children
is the number of healthy children who have been
affected by AIDS in that they are now orphans
because their parents have died from the disease. That
number is growing rapidly, but because the children
themselves are not infected, they are often overlooked.

When we talk about AIDS, we must talk about those who are infected and those who are affected. Because our concern is that there is a rapidly growing population of people who are affected by the AIDS crisis, and their needs are not being met, whether we're talking about helping them deal with the loss of a loved one, educating them, or whatever. And what we see is that when those people are adolescents, the concern is even greater because they are at risk even though they may be perfectly healthy. If their needs continue to go unmet, they in turn become at risk for contracting HIV themselves.

**Do you see a lot of those kinds of children?**
We do take in children who have been orphaned, and we have sometimes been criticized for doing that. For example, we once had a situation where we knew of a mother who had just gone into the hospital because she was very sick with AIDS. She had two young boys, one positive and one negative, and she had no one to care for them except for a home health aide who was afraid to be around the boy with HIV. We took both of the children into our home and tried to be supportive of them during the time that their mother was in the hospital. And we were criticized by a lot of people for taking in the HIV-negative child. But I think we can live with that kind of criticism.

**What is it like for a parent who has to give up a child to your care?**

It's very scary. I remember one day at one of our homes the doorbell rang. A nurse answered the door, and it was a mother standing there with a child by her side. She was obviously very frightened. She asked if this was the home for children with AIDS, and the nurse said it was. The mother then explained that she wanted to go into a drug treatment program but that she had nowhere to leave her child. The nurse reassured her that she had come to the right place, and that we would not try to take her child from her or refuse to give the child back once she finished her ninety-day program. So she left the child with us, and when she was finished with the program she came back and they were reunited. And that is a typical story.

What is becoming more and more common is that parents come to us who are in the last stages of AIDS-related illnesses and ask us to help them find a guardian for their children, someone who will care for them after the parents are gone.

**Is that hard to do?**

Right now it is very hard for parents to legally identify somebody to care for their children after their deaths, because in order to do that, they have to immediately give up all rights regarding the child. And this can often make parents feel even worse than they already do. Often, parents who are dying of AIDS stay alive simply because of their children. I can't tell you the number of times doctors have said to me that they didn't know why a particular person, usually a mother, was still alive when she should have been dead long ago. And it's usually because the mother is staying alive long enough to get the last details worked out in terms of finding a caregiver for her children.

**Do the children who come to you with HIV infection know what is going on with their health?**
I think they know more than we think they do sometimes, even if they don't know the specifics. I know one little girl who had been going for months to the hospital for treatments but had no idea why she was going. Then one day while she was playing outside, a cousin got angry at her and he blurted out that she had AIDS. She had no idea up until then. She knew she was sick, but she didn't know with what.

Denial is a natural part of this illness, not just for adults, but for children as well. So sometimes it's hard to know whether a child doesn't know or whether they are just in denial because they do know.

**Do a lot of the children feel like they are important only because they have AIDS?**
Yes, and what we've also found out is that many of the healthy siblings are forced into the background when

suddenly everything in the family revolves around the child with AIDS. Sometimes they feel guilty, as though they somehow did something wrong because they are healthy and a brother or sister isn't. The other experience is that the child with AIDS is getting a lot of attention, so anger builds up in the child who isn't. And that is perfectly natural and normal.

**It must also be tiring for children to always have to talk about AIDS.**
We have a project that we are working on now where we got people to give us space on billboards where we can put up artwork and writings done by the children in our programs. One child said, "I just don't want to do it. I'm tired of AIDS." This child is living in a home where both a nephew and a brother have AIDS. He is always surrounded by this. Part of teaching people how to cope with everything that AIDS brings with it is helping them to sometimes forget about AIDS for a few hours or minutes.

**How hard is it to find foster homes for children with HIV?**
There are a lot of people who are afraid to take in a child with HIV, and this includes relatives. There are a lot of people who would make wonderful foster parents, but because of fear they haven't taken in children with AIDS. We need to educate people so that they are not afraid. We recently had a grandmother

who did not want to take her HIV-infected grand-child because she was afraid of being near someone with the virus. She already had the child's sibling, but she was petrified of AIDS. Then she came to visit the child in our home, and she was completely over-whelmed by the love the child was receiving from our staff. When she saw them hugging and kissing her grandchild with absolutely no fear, it was the educa-tion that she needed to have so that she was able to take that child into her home and give him the love he needed.

**Does it make you angry when people have such fears?**
I understand those fears, because I know what I went through myself. I know what it's like to worry about what might happen if I work with children with AIDS or what might happen if my children's friends find out. There's a whole array of fears and concerns you have that you are afraid to express. So when I run into fear or prejudice about AIDS, I can remind myself what it was like for me, and hopefully I can help those people come to understand their fears.

**How did you overcome your fears?**
Something happened that I never, ever expected, and that was that every little thing I did for a child began to come back to me tenfold. It was unbelievable. I volunteered in a hospital before we opened the home.

I volunteered to open a playroom for children with AIDS who were spending hours at the clinic. And I was always trying to come up with new projects for them to do. When I saw the response to these projects, how much the children enjoyed them and how much their parents enjoyed them, it was a wonderful feeling. When I first started doing it, the response of some of the doctors and nurses was disbelief. They couldn't believe that I was actually going to go in there and work with these children with AIDS, was going to help them. But it was so spiritually rewarding for me. My husband says I would float into the house after spending a day with the kids, because I couldn't get over how much every little thing I did was appreciated.

I will never forget this one mother who was very ill. Her brother would bring the woman's child in every day. One day he couldn't, so she brought the child in herself. I still remember working with her and her daughter on a project, some little thing. Then the mother died, so the mother's girlfriend started bringing the child in. Sometime around Easter, the girlfriend was making a bunny out of cotton balls. The little girl was very sick by this time and was lying in the other room, dying. The girlfriend took the bunny into her room and placed it in bed with the girl. And I remember thinking how beautiful it was that she was doing exactly what the little girl's mother would have done, that she was continuing the life circle. That said so much to me about their friendship, and it's those kinds of experiences that people with AIDS have given me that no one else could ever give me.

**How do you deal with watching the children die?**
In many ways I am an administrator, so I am not with the children on a day-to-day basis where I can develop very close relationships with them. But there was one. Anyone involved in caregiving, particularly with children, knows that you are supposed to always keep yourself at a distance emotionally. But there's always one. Mine was the first child I knew with AIDS. I knew her from the days when I volunteered at the hospital. Then lo and behold, one day she became part of our program and became part of my life again.

Her death was extremely difficult, not just for me but for many people. She was one of the older children, and for some reason there was a period during the summer where a lot of the older children were dying. I saw that taking an unusual toll on the people in our program. And I think that that's because, no matter how well you know the facts or how much experience you have, in the back of your mind you convince yourself that there are certain kids who are going to beat it. So when these children began to die, it reminded us just how powerful AIDS really is. My special little friend was twelve when she died.

At the time, I honestly did not realize the toll her death was taking on me. I remember when the caseworker who had this child as part of her caseload came to me and told me that the doctors gave the child six months to live. I just took in the information and didn't think about it. What I didn't realize until much later was that I started withdrawing at that point because I didn't want to deal with her death. I actually had to take a leave of absence from the program because I felt so overwhelmed, even though I didn't really know why. It wasn't until after her death that I was able to regroup and come back. And even then it took me quite some time to realize that I had been responding to her death.

**How did you work through your feelings?**
It was the clients that helped get me through it. I remember being at the child's funeral. It rained that day, and I felt like I was totally at the end of my rope. I was crying like crazy. I looked up, and there was an HIV-positive woman. She had her child with her, and the woman threw her arms around me and tried to console me. I looked at her, and I thought, "This woman is dealing with AIDS. She is dealing with the fact that the child with her has AIDS. And here she is consoling me." It really moved me. She had brought her little girl, who also was HIV-infected, to say good-bye because she was very close to the girl who had died.

**What is it like for the children living with HIV to see the other children die?**

This little girl had asked to come to the funeral. I had a very special picture of the child who died, which she gave to me before she died. I had given her a puppy for Christmas, and she wanted to give me something special in return. She ran into her room and came back with a picture of herself as a baby. It was one of only two pictures that she owned. Both of them were of her as a baby, but one had her mother's hands in it propping her up. And she said she wanted me to have the one that included her mother's hands, because it was so special to her.

So I had copies of this picture made. At the funeral, I gave them to the child's grandmother, and she gave them out to special people in her life. One person who wanted one was this little girl, who had been her granddaughter's friend. After the little girl had viewed the body, I saw her walking along clutching the picture of her friend who was dead, and that was very, very special to me. It was important to her to come.

**How can you help children deal with seeing what might happen to them?**

I think you just have to listen. You never know what is important to children or why. One little girl told her foster mother that she wanted a picture of her mommy, who had died of AIDS. So they got a picture of the mother, and it had other people in it. And the child said that she wanted a picture of her mother all by herself. They got that. Every night, in the last stages of her life, this little girl would take that picture and put it at the top of her pillow so that it touched her head. And that's what she needed to do in order to be able to sleep.

She had created her own ritual, and it's important to recognize the significance of rituals. We have a summer camp for families dealing with AIDS, and often it's very hard for families to go back there when someone in the family has died during the year. It's hard for them to go to a place where they used to laugh and have fun together. So now we have ceremonies that help families heal, like letting balloons go or planting a tree to remember the person who has died.

**How do your own children react to your work?**
They've all been involved on some level. Our oldest daughter just graduated from college with a degree in public policy, and she is working for an AIDS organization, finding resources for homeless, drug-addicted people with AIDS. So there is definitely something there that is a result of what her parents do. My son's love is acting and video making. He is a junior in high school. A project that he is working on now is to videotape a memorial for a woman who is HIV-positive and wants something for her young

twins to remember her by when she is gone. So he is going to film her and prepare this tape for her to give to her children. I think that will be an incredible experience for him.

**And your youngest has grown up with this?**
She is ten, so she has been surrounded by the AIDS crisis her whole life. I see it affecting her in a very positive way. She is a very sensitive, spontaneous person, and she is very loving. She helped me get through the death of the child I was close to. She was the same age, and they had been friends, and she kept reminding me when I would get sad what a fighter that little girl had been and how proud I should be of her for fighting so hard. She just loves life. I was just asked to be a speaker at her school for career day, and when she found out, she turned to me and said, "And of course you will do it." So I'm glad to see that what we do is important to her.

**What is the hardest part of what you do?**
When we first got involved, we had no idea just how many children and families were being affected by the AIDS crisis. We saw the child with AIDS, the homeless child with AIDS, and the fact that this child had a limited life expectancy, and we wanted to give that child as much as we could for as long as that child had to live. At that time, that was what we saw. But since then, we have been spun in so many different direc-

tions that at times I feel like our client has actually become the whole world. There are so many needs when it comes to the effects of AIDS that it is impossible to narrow the groups you're reaching out to down to one. There are children living with HIV, children whose parents are living with HIV, relatives, friends, and the unconcerned.

It's hard to find where you fit and to determine whether or not you are living up to your responsibilities. Because you know that you won't be here forever and can't do it all. And that whole thing is very hard. I can't tell you how many people have found out about us and asked us for help in opening homes. We help everyone we can. But you can't do everything. And you can't let that immobilize you, because then you become a part of the problem, another victim of HIV/AIDS.

It seems like it's a never-ending circle that keeps expanding. I had the opportunity to go to Russia, and at first I thought there was nothing I could do there. Then I got there, and I looked into the eyes of the Russian mothers, and I realized that their needs and concerns are the same as those of mothers here. That can be overwhelming, if you take all of that seriously and feel that you have an obligation to all of these people. Because you want to help everybody, but you can't do it all.

**What is the most rewarding part of what you do?**

I hope that I'm always touched and can always feel the results of little acts, whether it's bringing a child a puppy or coloring eggs for the first time with a child who might not get to color eggs again next year. Just the little things. I hope I'm always able to see them and appreciate them as worth their weight in gold, because they are worth that, and more.

# AIDS FAST FACT NUMBER *Six*

## What Is Safer Sex?

*Safer sex* is a term used to describe sexual activities that are at low risk for the transmission of HIV.

Because any sex at all with another person is potentially risky, the only one hundred percent sure way to avoid exposure to HIV through sex is to abstain, or not have any sex at all. And in fact, more and more people do not have sex until they have found someone they want to spend their lives with and are sure that person is also HIV-negative.

But at some point, most people will begin having sex. So if you decide that abstinence is not right for you, you must always practice safer sex. There are many sexual things you can do more safely, and some of them include:

• anal or vaginal intercourse during which the man's penis is covered by a latex condom, or rubber. Condoms for women, which are inserted into the vagina, are also available, but they are expensive and often awkward to use.

- oral sex in which the man's penis is covered by a latex condom, or oral sex where the woman's vaginal area is covered by a sheet of latex rubber called a dental dam or by a piece of ordinary plastic wrap. A dental dam is a square of rubber that is held over the opening of the vagina to provide a barrier between a woman's vaginal fluids and her partner's mouth or tongue.

- kissing and hugging. Not all sex has to involve the sex organs. Sometimes it can be more pleasurable for partners just to touch each other's bodies or give each other back rubs or massages.

- masturbating your partner when neither of you has cuts or sores on your hands or fingers. Just getting someone's semen or vaginal fluids on your skin cannot infect you. The fluids have to come into direct contact with your bloodstream through cuts or open sores. Of course, masturbating yourself poses no danger of contracting HIV.

- rubbing against each other to the point of orgasm

- talking. Yes, talking. Tell your partner what you like about her or him. Talk about your dreams and what you want for the future. Talk about what you like and don't like, whether it's about sex or something else.

These are only some of the safe things you can do. Use your imagination and you'll probably think of a lot more. While some people say that safer sex is a turnoff, or that it is too hard to use condoms, it can be fun and exciting to find new ways to make love. If you try to find different ways to make sex safer, you will probably find that it also makes it a lot more enjoyable, because you are showing that you care enough about yourself and your partner to protect you both from contracting HIV.

## Penny Raife Durant

# A WRITER'S WORDS

*When a close friend told her he had AIDS, writer Penny Raife Durant needed a way to help her sort out her feelings about his illness. She decided to write a book about someone dealing with the effects of AIDS. The result was her 1992 novel* When Heroes Die, *the story of Gary, a young man who discovers that his adored uncle Rob has AIDS.* When Heroes Die *was one of the first books to deal with the effects of the AIDS crisis on the lives of young people, and it won a Lambda Literary Award for best children's book.*

**Tell me about the friend who prompted you to write this book.**

Billy was one of my husband, Omar's, best friends growing up in a small town in New Mexico. After we were married, I met him and we spent a lot of time together. He was a wonderful friend to both of us. Then he moved away to California. When he came back to visit, he would always take my kids out and buy them the thing that Mom wouldn't let them have and take them to all these great places. So they knew him as Uncle Billy, although he wasn't a blood relation.

One summer when he came to see us, he walked in the door and very cryptically said that he had come to meet with his aunt and uncle. He had a sister and nephews, but both of his parents had died, and his aunt and uncle were all that was left of his older-aged family. And my husband said, "That sounds pretty ominous," to which Billy replied, "Well, it is for me." Then he said he would call us the next day and walked out the door, leaving us sitting there. And somehow I just knew that he had AIDS. I didn't know how I knew, but I knew. And when he came back the next day, he told us that was what it was, and we were able to talk about it.

**Did it make it easier for him that you knew?**
Yes, it did. He thought that it was going to be hard to tell his family, because he had never told them he was gay. But they were very wonderful to him, and that relieved a lot of the burden. We'd all watched and worried about him from the moment the AIDS epidemic started.

Then he went back to Los Angeles, and there was

nothing I could do, because I was too far away. You know, I could call, and I wrote him letters and sent him cards. But it wasn't enough. There was a piece of my life and my husband's life and my children's lives that was dying. And I wanted Billy to move back here with us. We talked about it, and my oldest son was willing to give up his bedroom and share with his younger brother so that we could take care of Billy here. He wanted to come, but he really needed the number of gay men and the number of other people living with AIDS that Los Angeles had, as well as the medical knowledge and facilities. He stayed there so that he wouldn't feel alone.

**He never came to live with you?**
No, he didn't. But he came to visit. One of the things that he wanted to do most before he died was go to a University of New Mexico Lobos basketball game. He said, "I just have to hear that roar one more time." It's almost impossible to get tickets to a Lobos game when they're playing here on their own court. But some friends of ours gave up their tickets for us, and we got to go to three basketball games while he was here. My husband went out to see him later that year, and it turned out to be the last time. Billy died a few months later.

**How did your boys react to his illness?**
Adam was only seven or eight at the time, so he

didn't react much at all. Geoff was twelve, and when Billy came to visit, I told Geoffrey that I would like for Billy to sleep in his room, and was that okay with him. I explained to him that there was nothing to worry about, and that he could not get AIDS just by sleeping in the same room that someone with AIDS had slept in. We discussed all his concerns. I was really proud when he said that it was fine with him. He was never afraid of Billy.

When I finished the first draft of the manuscript, I made copies and had Geoffrey's science class read it. Then I went in and talked to them about AIDS and about writing. It was fascinating to sit with a roomful of very intelligent middle schoolers and get their opinions.

**What did they think?**
Some of them thought that they wouldn't have read the book if they hadn't had to. And they were honest, which I appreciated. One girl told me that she would never have picked that book off the shelf, because she didn't like the title. I think that she just didn't want to read something about death, and it tells you right in the title that someone is going to die.

There was only one boy who said that if a man walked into the room and he knew that the man was gay, he would run out the door. That was a reaction I wasn't anticipating, and I was surprised by it. So we were able to talk about it a little bit, and I think that was good for everyone.

I was willing to answer any questions they had, and because I wasn't their mother, they asked me all kinds of questions. One girl had obviously been very concerned about her father because her father's girlfriend lived in a house with three women who were lesbians. She was afraid that he would get AIDS because they were gay. This is how little she knew, and it reminded me just how much kids need information about AIDS.

**Did you ever think that you would be writing about AIDS, or think that it would have an effect on your life?**

No, I didn't. I didn't think so at all. It wasn't until AIDS came into our lives and, at the same time, I had a young adolescent of my own and realized how little he knew and how little all of us knew at that point, that I really saw how important it was for that age group to be informed.

**Were you surprised that there weren't more books for young people about AIDS?**

When I was working on the book, I read all of the books for young people that were available then, which was only two. One was M. E. Kerr's *Night Kites,* and the other was about a boy who contracted the virus through a blood transfusion. While these were both good books, I really felt that the sexual issue had to be addressed, so that was also part of why I wrote my book.

**How has your experience with AIDS changed the way you talk with your own children about it?**
I can tell you that there is a big difference between how I have talked with them about it. With Geoffrey, it was always a "just say no" kind of approach, which I now realize doesn't do any good at all. I don't think that is an effective way to deal with ninety percent of the kids.

With Adam, who is fourteen and has grown up with AIDS all around him, I have taken a much more informed approach. Recently, there was an item on the news, and we were all watching it together. It was about whether or not the health clinics in high schools should be allowed to dispense condoms. Well, I'm one of the people who say that they should definitely be allowed.

So we talked a little bit, and what I had to say to Adam was, "I would rather you wait. I would rather that you find the person you're going to be with forever and have a monogamous relationship. But I also know that may not be realistic, and I would rather have you be protected and safe than maintain a sense of innocence that is artificial."

That was hard. I really didn't know how to say it to him. And he said, "I'm just going to say this once.

Now you just listen. I don't intend to have sex before marriage. But if something would happen and I would decide that I was going to have sex before marriage, I would use a condom." And I said, "That's wonderful. I'm very proud of you."

This was not the discussion I had with my older son, where I had just said no. And I think it was hard for both of us to say those things, especially for Adam to talk to me about sex.

**How hard is it being a parent and talking about AIDS with a child?**
I felt fairly certain that Adam was not having sex. But it is hard to admit the possibility that your child could be sexually active, or will be within a few years. Next year he will be going to high school, and the pressures there will be very different than they are now.

**What is it like knowing that your child is going out into a world where loving someone else could potentially kill him?**
I'm a child of the 1960s. I started college in 1969, and that was a time when the only concern was whether or not you would get pregnant from having sex. And because of the pill, that was not much of a concern. This is a very different concern. And it's hard to say that times were different then, or that it was okay then and isn't now. But I think

that we were just more open about sexuality then.

There has always been premarital sex; it's just that now it's become deadly. And it's frightening. There are a lot of things in the world that can be frightening. I guess that's where our responsibility as parents comes in—to let our children know the dangers and what they can do about them. Then, at that point, you have to let go and trust that they will make the correct decisions. And sometimes they do, and sometimes they don't. And that's very hard to watch. You want to walk around behind them and tap them on the shoulder every time they do anything that could be dangerous.

I'm sure that especially for young men who are going through that time of questioning their sexual orientation and who believe that they are gay, AIDS adds another huge burden and level of fear. Loving should be the one thing we do that we do right and do well. And it's scary now. You shouldn't have to worry about dying when you're thirteen or fourteen years old.

**What has the response to *When Heroes Die* been when you speak with young people who have read it?**
They have a lot of questions. I realize that the book probably raises more questions than it answers, which is fine with me. It was not intended to be a textbook about AIDS, but a story. First and foremost, I want-

ed it to be a story in which the kids cared about Gary and his relationship with his uncle. So they have a lot of questions about AIDS and about being gay, which I try to answer as honestly as I possibly can when I speak to them.

One student teacher in a classroom of sixth graders thought it was an inappropriate book to read to the kids. The teacher asked him why he thought that. He said he thought they were too young to talk about these issues. So when I went to speak to that class, he had a lot of questions that I was able to answer. And by talking to him, I was able to remove some of his own fears about the subject.

**Do you think adults are more frightened of your book than young people?**
I think that's probably true. One mother called the teacher of a class that had read my book and said, "What are you reading to my daughter? She came home asking me questions after she'd read that book." I think she was one of those people who think that if you don't talk about it, it won't affect your life. Which just isn't true. When people don't want to talk about something, it's usually because they are afraid of it. So when you educate them, you make it easier to talk about it.

**It must be very fulfilling to know that your book has opened up so much discussion.**

I think that's a very strong benefit that I get from having written the book, especially when someone tells me that they read the book or their child read the book and started asking questions. I think we have to get kids asking questions, because there's too much information that they need that they're not going to get unless they really want it. And it has to come before it's too late. You don't want to tell them about these things after they've started experimenting sexually. They've got to know before that.

**What was it like for you writing the book?**
I started off writing the book thinking I was writing it for Billy's nephews and for my children, and I discovered that I was really writing it for me. It ended up being my way of doing something to cope with Billy's illness and then his death. It was an interesting process, because for fiction I don't normally do a lot of research. But this needed a lot of research. I wanted it to be accurate, because I wanted it to raise questions. I wanted kids to get some information from the book as well as a story.

When I write fiction, I start by interviewing my characters. I sit down at the computer and I start to ask them questions. They tell me their backgrounds, and they tell me what they like. Then we get started on the story. And the voices come through. And usually by the second or third page of these interviews, I have the character's voice.

**Was it a healing process for you?**
I think it was definitely a healing process. It made me focus on loss, and what happens when someone we love dies. My father had died in 1986, but he had been sick for two years before he died, and we had a long time to say good-bye. I didn't get that time with Billy. I think writing the book was a way to be involved with Billy as I wrote, even though he was not here. I could be more involved with his life and his death because of my involvement with the story.

I must have needed that because I was not able to convince him to come here and be with us. I could have taken care of him, and done it very well, but I would never have written this book if I had done that. I wouldn't have felt like I had to write it then. And perhaps this is a better legacy, because I wouldn't have been able to keep him from dying. And now, if this book keeps one kid safe or makes one kid think about it enough to ask the questions and get the information she or he needs not to get AIDS, then it's worth it.

## *Seven*

# What about Oral Sex?

One of the biggest areas of concern for young people is oral sex. Oral sex is when a man puts his penis in his partner's mouth or a woman's partner inserts his or her tongue into the woman's vagina.

A lot of people assume that oral sex is okay because a man is not putting his penis into his partner's vagina or rectum. Unfortunately, that's not true. While oral sex is often considered to be one of the lower-risk sexual acts, it is still possible for HIV to be transmitted that way. The AIDS virus can pass through even tiny cuts on your gums or tongue, so if these cuts are exposed to your partner's vaginal fluids, blood, or semen during oral sex, you could become infected.

It's also important to remember that a man usually will secrete fluid from his penis when sexually aroused, even if he doesn't come. This fluid, called precome, can contain the AIDS virus. So just because a man does not ejaculate into his partner's mouth during oral sex does not mean that his partner is not being exposed to HIV.

To protect themselves and their partners during oral sex, a man should always wear a latex condom and a woman should always use a dental dam, which provides a barrier against HIV. While rubber might not taste very good, it is the only way to prevent the transmission of HIV. If you put flavored lotions or creams on a condom or dental dam to make it taste good, don't use chocolate or any oil-based substances, as they can weaken rubber and cause it to rip.

# _Philippa Lawson_

# TAKING IT TO THE STREETS

_When Philippa Lawson was five years old, in 1968, her family had to flee their home in Czechoslovakia when the Russians invaded. The family moved to the United States looking for a safer life. But for Philippa, life was not happy. She spent her teenage years dealing with a poor self-image and the feeling that life was not worth living. At eighteen, she found herself in the last place that she ever expected to be—living on the streets and working as a prostitute to support her drug habit. For five years she endured the harsh life faced by people involved in prostitution. Finally, through family intervention, she was helped to get off the streets. Unfortunately, she also found out that she was HIV-positive._

_It is easy for some of us to look down on people involved in prostitution. But for some women and men in the United States, including thou-_

*sands of young people, prostitution is the only way they know of to stay alive. Many of them are supporting children, and many are abused both physically and emotionally by people who force them to prostitute themselves to make money. And because unsafe sex and drug use are common in the world of prostitution, many of these people are now living with the added threat of HIV infection.*

*Seven years after getting off the streets, Philippa Lawson is still involved in prostitution, but as an HIV/AIDS counselor and educator. As the director of the HIV Health Program of Chicago's Genesis House, she works with the working prostitutes in that city to educate them about the dangers of HIV and AIDS. By reaching out to the community of which she was once a member, Philippa is offering hope to a group of people forgotten by traditional social service agencies but not overlooked by the AIDS epidemic.*

**How was Genesis House founded?**
Genesis House was founded by Edwina Gateley, a British human rights worker, who started it because she felt a calling from God. In the 1970s, she had founded an organization called the Voluntary Missionary Movement. She had worked with them for a number of years and was doing a retreat all alone in the woods by herself, trying to find out where she

would be directed next. She had a spiritual experience that led her to help the prostitution community. She had no experience with this group, but she felt called to help them because she felt they are one of the groups most ignored by the churches. So she started Genesis House ten years ago, and it's just grown from there.

**What did she do?**
She just walked the streets of Chicago for months, learning who the community was. Then she found a house, and it all took off from there. Now we have two locations. The original is on the North Side, across from Wrigley Field. We also have a satellite on the West Side, which is another rough area. The North Side home can house up to six women. We also offer crisis sheltering to anyone who needs it, and we offer group counseling. People can come in for food or clothing, or just to take a shower. Our creed is to love people and accept people no matter where they are in their lives. We certainly hope that people will want to get out of prostitution because of the pain of the streets. But if they don't, any kind of positive change in their lives is wonderful. Just coming in for a shower is a big step for these women.

**Are a lot of the women you work with still involved in prostitution?**
Most of them are. We see six thousand women a year

on the streets and in the courts. We also have non-residential services for people who are out of prostitution. They come for Prostitutes Anonymous and counseling and other things. I work on a project called the HIV Health Program. We say *health* because everyone associates HIV and AIDS with death, when really it encompasses many different issues related to living.

**Is your personal story a typical one for women on the street?**
Most women start young like I did, or younger. The difference is that most of them don't get out. I got out when I was twenty-three. Most women don't get out. Most women die. Those that are fortunate enough to get out are normally in their midthirties. But that's just an average. We get women anywhere from sixteen to their midsixties coming to us for help. I was extremely fortunate that once I admitted to my family I had a problem, they cared and loved me enough that they wanted to help me.

**How did you get off the streets?**
I had been raped three times in the period of a few months. The fourth time, a man had me trapped in a van and was raping me. I had an out-of-body experience where I saw myself from above, and I saw that my whole life had been about pain. And suddenly I was filled with this determination to live. It was the

first time in my life that I can remember really want-
ing to live. I somehow fought him off and got out of
the van. I ran down the street naked and screaming
and bleeding.

**And you decided to get help?**
After finally admitting to my family I had a problem
with drugs, I entered a detox program on January 1,
1987. I was fortunate in that my family was able to
get me into a hospital and get drug treatment at
that time. A lot of people on the streets are not
that lucky. Most people do not have families that
can or want to help. I remember calling drug
treatment centers in New York City, where I was
living, from pay phones on the street and being
told that there was a waiting list of six months
to a year. They said that if I had six hundred dollars,
I could get into a program right away. And there
I was, a woman living on the streets. I couldn't even
buy toilet paper, so there was no way I could afford to
pay for treatment. People forget that prostitutes and
other people living on the streets don't have insurance
and can't just go to the doctor or the hospital when
they want to. People say, "Why don't they just get
help?" Well, first you have to decide that you're
worth helping, which is hard enough. Then you have
to find someone who can help you, which is just as
hard. For many people, it's easier just to stay on the
streets.

**How did you find out that you were HIV-positive?**
I found out I was HIV-positive after I got off the streets, which is different from the experiences of many people in prostitution, who go back out onto the streets after they find out because they still have to earn a living. When I entered treatment, I demanded that I be tested. They didn't want to do it.

**Why not?**
Because no one had ever been tested. In New York in 1987, five years after the AIDS crisis began, they still didn't think drug addicts should be tested, because we wouldn't be able to stay sober and we'd just go back out on the streets because we couldn't deal with the fact that we had the virus. They didn't know how to counsel someone who was HIV-positive. They sat on the results for a month and a half, until the day I was shipped out to Chicago to the halfway house where I would finish my program. The counselors were crying and everything.

**What was your reaction?**
At that time, they couldn't really tell you that much about HIV and AIDS, especially about how it affected women. What they said was that I could be dead—a fifty-fifty chance—within two years. So I left for Chicago thinking that I was going to die any day.

When I got to Chicago, it was even worse. I was

from New York. I was a prostitute. I was a junkie. And I was HIV-positive. I had been on the streets, and I was sent to a halfway house in a suburb of Chicago. Most of the people there were wealthy, and cocaine addiction was the problem. So there was a lot of prejudice there. In fact, they told me not to talk about it to anyone. The same thing about being raped. They told me not to talk about it. I was having flashbacks, and I thought I was going to die. So all of these things were going on, and I had no one to talk to. Those experiences are what motivated me to help others.

**How did all of this make you feel?**
I knew there was this virus inside me, but there was no lab work they could do for me. I had so much shame to begin with, and it made me feel even more ashamed that I was told not to tell anyone my story. I also had rage from the streets, so I was angry. But the most overwhelming experience was just being grateful for being alive and enjoying every moment of being alive. I knew the pain of the streets, and I knew that if I only had two years to live, I wanted to live in a way that was very different.

I had a lot of issues, like body-image issues and compulsive overeating. When people would point out that I was a woman, I would get really, really upset, especially if anyone was attracted to me. First, I had shame about my prostitution past. Then, with

HIV, I wrote off ever having sex again. Again, though, this motivated me to help start an HIV support group.

**Did that group help you deal with your feelings?**
It was a mixed thing. There was a small group of us at first, and that group grew. They were my foundation. But I was the only one in the group who believed that you don't have to die from HIV. I will eventually die, but there's never been a disease that is one hundred percent fatal, and no one knows if all of us are going to die from HIV. I don't know if I'll be the one to live or not, but I don't have to believe that I'm going to be dead in two years. And I watched people then who believed the media's message that everyone with HIV died right away, and I see people who believe it now, and those are the people who are dying. When you believe you are going to get sick, you do.

**Why did you bring your story public?**
It became very draining for me, because everyone in my support group was focused on dying, and I felt that there was a strong need to live. So what I started doing was speaking a lot in high schools, talking about my teenage years and what I went through. No one could believe I was doing it—that I was actually telling my story—because everyone else I knew with HIV, especially women, was dealing with it alone and in silence. But I couldn't do that, because I knew that

shame over it was not helpful. I just didn't want people to be alone with it.

Four years ago, that same halfway house I had first been in in Chicago asked me to come and speak to the staff about AIDS/HIV education. And there in the room was the doctor I'd had there. I was sitting next to him, and he didn't even recognize me. This was a man who had done nothing for me. I was his first patient with HIV. And he started talking to the group about his first patient, and I turned to him and said, "Do you realize that I am that patient?" And he started apologizing for not recognizing me, and he was telling me how far they'd come since then. And my response was, "Good, because you really needed to."

**What is the hardest part of your job?**
The hardest part of my job is seeing what happens to kids. That's been so hard, seeing the cycle of violence and despair being repeated over and over on the streets. Those teenage years were so painful for me. I was obsessed with suicide; I had tried to kill myself three times. Most of my life I felt like life was just way too hard and I was incapable of doing it. I just wanted out. And when you're a teenager, people are all around you telling you that these are the best years of your life, and you're thinking that if they're the best, then you don't want to see the worst. I always felt like there was no one I could ask for help, and I think a

lot of young people go through that.

At that time, my family had a lot of problems, and I felt like I had to take those problems on too. I never told my family that I was on the streets. I made up this whole lie so that they wouldn't know, for five years. For teenagers, there's just this terrible burden of being alone, of not being accepted anywhere. And for many kids, they are dealing with issues of sexual, mental, or physical abuse, or maybe with their own sexuality. I always tell young people, find someone you can talk to or ask for help, whether it's a teacher or a friend or whoever. Because it's so sad to see people die in tragic ways when you know that if only someone had known the pain these people were in, it could have been avoided. With young people, it really is reality that a lot of their problems are coming from their families. So that makes it even harder to get help. And there's not always an easy solution.

**How has your life changed the most since you left the streets?**
Being given HIV and told that I might die, but remembering my desire to live while that man was trying to kill me, really changed my life around. I'd seen death and poverty. So death was not this big, scary thing. It was life I knew nothing about. So that became my mission—to find out about life. To get a bike! I never thought I would have a bike, or the energy to ride it. Now I'm so into riding my bike so that

I feel like I'm flying. That's something I never thought I could do.

It's now been eight years for me. And every year the statistics on long-term survivors give me another year to live, so who knows. No one's in charge of my life except me and my belief in a universal higher power. And when I'm done, I'm done. I don't care if it's HIV or getting hit by a bus. When I found out, I really believed that I might die in the morning. So when people would hug me, it was like I'd never experienced a hug before. I would start getting real emotional. Or when I'd see something beautiful, I'd get all teary-eyed because I felt like I'd never see it again. Now I work two jobs, I have a life, I have a car. My appointment book is filled. I am living.

**Do you ever feel like you just don't want to do this anymore?**
I'm working with a lot of people who don't want help, for whatever reason, whether it's HIV or prostitution or drug use. And a lot of them die out there on the streets. I have to accept that, because everyone is in their own place. But I do at times feel burned out. It's been five years now that I've been doing this. I would like to do something where I'm working with people who are looking to live with HIV, not living in despair because of it.

**Does speaking help you deal with it?**

Actually, I usually say no to interviews, because now there are so many people out there living with HIV, and each one of them has a story to tell. I am not the only one. Other people need their turn. It takes a lot to share your life. It's always draining for me, no matter how uplifting it is.

My life is no longer just HIV. My life is my life. I just happen to be HIV-positive. And yes, I happen to have worked the streets as a prostitute. And yes, I was strung out on heroin and cocaine. But that's not all of me. HIV is just a little virus that I happen to have that might kill me or might not. But that's not who Philippa is.

**Was it hard to get to that point?**
Yes. That's why I do other things now besides my AIDS work. I try to balance my life. Because I was obsessed with HIV for a long time. And that isn't healthy. All of your phone calls are about HIV. Anyone who comes up positive, a lot of friends will refer them to me. So it really can take over your life. I'm just now learning how to say no to all of these things. And that's been one of the hardest things. Because on one hand, I want to talk to everyone that I can and educate them. But I need time for me.

**What do you do through Genesis House?**
We hire women who have been involved in prostitu-

tion to be AIDS educators. A lot of times, it's their first job. So it gives them a lot of self-confidence. They have to have been out of prostitution for at least a year. Many of them are just getting their children back and just getting their lives back together, so it's sometimes hard for them.

We go out and walk the strolls, the areas where the prostitutes work. We work in teams of two women, and we wear badges so that the women know who we are. We answer questions, and we hand out information. We educate women about HIV and other sexually transmitted diseases. We tell them that if they ever need help, they can come to us. We also hand out condoms and bleach for cleaning needles.

We also work with the partners of women involved in prostitution, because the majority of women don't use condoms with their significant others. They will use them with their customers, but not with their own partners, because with prostitution some of these women are having sex ten times a day. When they then go back to their main partner, to have sex again with that person needs to somehow be different, so that they don't feel like they are with a trick. Usually what that means is not using a condom. But a lot of these male partners inject drugs and sleep with other people, so the women who have miraculously escaped becoming infected by customers are being infected by their own partners.

**Do the workers who go onto the streets encounter any hostility?**

Our main purpose is to build relationships. So if there is a new woman, usually a teenager, on the street, she will usually have an older man standing on the corner watching her to make sure she doesn't run away. So a lot of times, you have to ask permission from the older man to talk to the woman. And that's incredibly hard to do if you're a woman and you're working through these shame issues anyway. But if you don't, you know that the woman you talk to will get hurt by the man later. The educators are open about their pasts in prostitution, so they can tell the women that they know what's going on because they've been there. A lot of our workers are known from the streets, so they have an in.

Over time, we develop relationships with the women out there. At first, they might just want condoms and don't want to talk. But in order for them to get condoms, we make them listen to the education part of our speech. And sometimes we only have a minute or two because the woman has a customer waiting. But we tell her what we can. We also do court outreach, so we see them in the courts and in the jails. We see them everywhere. So eventually they come to see that we really do care about them.

We always invite them to Genesis House to get food and clothes or drug treatment. There's a big problem with people who don't have insurance getting medical help. So naturally that rules out the entire prostitution community. So we offer them treatment services that they can't get other places. Also, many of these women have children, and often we will get them coming in just to talk about their kids. The issue with people who have not been involved in this life is that they just don't know the pain it involves, and they can be very judgmental. But our educators have been there, and they know how hard it is. Even then, it's hard. Because it's easy for a woman who has been there and gotten out to look at women who are still in it and be angry that they aren't trying harder to get themselves out. So we do a lot of training about accepting people where they are.

**Is it hard not to get angry when women don't want your help?**
It is hard, especially when you know and you see so obviously the pain of the street and you know what it's like to feel hopeless. And that's why we try to instill hope in these people. To change on your own is almost impossible, but there is always hope. For me, I was just hopeless on the street. I thought that there was no way out and that I was just going to die out there. Maybe if someone had come to me and told me about Genesis House and said that there was a place where I could get what I needed, I might not be HIV-infected.

**Do the women involved in prostitution know about HIV?**

Women involved in prostitution are pretty educated about HIV. Some are extremely educated, to the point where they know a lot of the scientific aspects relating to HIV and AIDS. The majority of people know how it is transmitted and how to prevent transmission. This isn't to say that they are practicing those measures, but they do know about them. What they don't know about is the fact that there is hope about HIV, that there is life after HIV. They don't know that it doesn't mean that you have AIDS, and that you're not going to die immediately just because you're HIV-positive.

Even within the AIDS community there is emphasis on dying. One of the big AIDS activism slogans is AIDS=DEATH. Granted, a lot of people die, and I don't want to take away from that. But let's accept it and talk about all of the things that you can do with HIV. I get angry, because every HIV training I go to, they talk about death and dying. We need to talk about living, also. Most people with HIV have never had a chance to live their lives, whether they're gay or drug abusers or whatever. Most people with HIV are dealing with shame issues, because somewhere someone has made them feel that there is something wrong with them. We need to talk to people with HIV about getting apartments, about getting child care, about how to live their lives in a totally different way than they ever have before.

## How do you deal with the death aspect of your work?

Every time someone dies, you go through it all over again. Last month, four of my friends died. My whole support group has died. It got to the point where I didn't want any more friends who were HIV-positive. But of course, my life had another thing in mind. Now I have all of these close friends with HIV. I've been romantically involved with people with HIV. And then, I go through what other people go through as I watch them freak out about getting symptoms, watching them get diseases, and all of that. And it's really scary. When you have one friend after another die, you don't have time to go through the grieving process for each one. My mother is a concentration camp survivor, and I really look at the AIDS crisis as being like the Holocaust, as a whole group of people dying one after the other with no end in sight.

## What is the attitude toward the prostitution community?

Many people feel that it is still acceptable to look down on prostitutes, and especially prostitutes with HIV. Even within the AIDS community there is that feeling. This is why I work at Genesis House. You would think that for people who deal with women's issues, prostitution would be something they know about and are caring about. But many don't. For a lot of people who are involved in prostitution, take away the drugs and prostitution, and they don't know anything else. That's their only way of getting finances. And it's also a kind of way to get love.

I think it's easier, if you're HIV infected, to say that you're an IV drug user, at least if you're a man. If you're a woman, that's harder, because people for some reason think it's worse for women to use drugs than for men. But in general, it's easier to say you have a problem with drugs. To say that you're involved in prostitution puts a whole other label on you. The majority of our staff will not talk about being in prostitution when they go to support groups, because they feel ashamed of it and embarrassed by it.

When I talk, I normally reveal my past with prostitution and doing it to get money for drugs. Afterward, women come up to me and tell me that they've been there too, and were afraid to tell anyone. And friends of mine say, "Well, I slept with a whole lot of people I met in bars, and I don't know their names. How does that make me any different from you just because I didn't ask for money?" And that's exactly right. Prostitution is trading sex for something else. It doesn't matter if it's money or a drink at a bar or whatever.

But people are still discriminated against for being involved in prostitution. This is not a moral issue. Even women or men who have been raped on the streets and try to press charges are told it wasn't really rape because somehow they deserved it or wanted it because they were prostitutes. And women especially internalize that. As a woman on the street, rape and sexual abuse are just part of life. If you survive and you live, that's wonderful. But if you're found in a Dumpster, that's part of life too. But women on the streets take on that attitude and begin to say, "Well, maybe I deserve it."

**Do people in the AIDS community do it too?**
Yes. There is a kind of AIDS hierarchy, with babies being at the top. It's easiest to feel sorry for babies who are infected, because obviously they didn't do anything to get HIV. Everyone else falls under that depending on how they were infected. We frequently like to feel sorry for people based on how much they can be "blamed" for having their disease. Prostitutes are easy for people to blame because people feel that they somehow asked for HIV by sleeping with people.

That's happening right now in the prostitution community. The attitude is, "You should have known better." Even myself, I've felt it when I see people who are out of the working life and are still going and having unsafe sex. I've had to work through that. When I was infected, we really didn't know it was a possibility to get infected. I practiced safer sex with all my customers, except one man. And I never shared needles, again except for with this one man. I thought I was safe, because I had been involved with him for five years. And look what happened.

**How does this affect the women who are counselors?**
They are finding their worth. I always say outreach is the hardest job you will ever have, and I really believe that. This is a stepping-stone, and they can move on from there. So that's one thing. They're finding out that they're not such awful people, that there are a lot of people out there like them, who are or have worked in prostitution.

They're also working through their own issues, like forming relationships. We are all women working in the office, and being around other women who are changing their lives for the better has to have an effect on you. So really, it's about changing your life. The one thing I hear from a lot of the women is that they never thought that they could ever give anything to anyone, and by working to help others like themselves, they find that, despite the fact that they might not have education or degrees or whatever, they are giving other women hope because they can give them their stories.

It's amazing that out of all this pain and out of all this garbage can come this beautiful flower. And they can do something that no one else can do. No one can say to someone else, "I've been there," when they haven't been there. Intellectually you can understand, but for someone who's still out there, it's very important that the person talking to her can say, "I do know what it's like because I've been here on this corner."

For most of these women, no one's ever asked them about themselves, and they've been treated as scum for as long as they can remember. And now they're respected. First it comes from outside, from others on the job. Then, eventually, it starts to come from inside as they learn to respect themselves.

**What's the most important thing we can tell people about AIDS?**
AIDS education is going to have to become showing people how to love themselves. Because no one is going to change their behavior until they love themselves. Telling a person to use a condom does nothing if that person does not respect and love her- or himself.

Also, the slogan We Are All Affected by HIV is absolutely true, though some of us are still in denial. I think HIV is here on our planet at this time to teach us to break down the judgments and barriers that we have toward people who are somehow different from us. HIV can teach us that we all have areas of shame, hurt, and abandonment. Yet, through admitting our secrets, we become powerful. By dealing with death on a daily basis, we can learn the true importance of the gift of life. Life is short, and our focus must be learning how to love ourselves, which in turn leads us to helping, through loving, others.

*Author's Note: Shortly before this book was published, Philippa Lawson left Genesis House to become the director of the HIV Community Coalition, an HIV/AIDS advocacy group based in Washington, D.C. The first AIDS organization staffed almost entirely by people living with HIV, the HCC is a unique new voice in the fight against AIDS. "I followed my dream of working with other HIV-positive people who are committed to living," Philippa says of her new job with this grassroots organization.*

# AIDS FAST FACT NUMBER
## *Eight*

## Fact & Fiction

When it comes to HIV, there are a lot of rumors and myths going around. Believing these myths can be a big mistake. They can also make you more afraid than you need to be, so it's important to know the truth.

Some of the most common myths about HIV are:

*Pulling the penis out before ejaculating will prevent the transmission of HIV.*
Even before a man ejaculates, or comes, his penis produces a liquid that can contain HIV. If any of this liquid comes in contact with your bloodstream, you can be infected.

*You can't get HIV if you're having your period.*
In fact, there might not be a better time. It's very easy for the AIDS virus to pass through the thin skin of the vaginal walls, and during a woman's period a lot

of her blood vessels are swollen and very close to the skin's surface, providing a greater area for HIV to enter the body. Also, since HIV is always found in the blood of an infected person, an infected woman can easily infect her partner if her blood comes into contact with cuts or sores on her partner's penis, tongue, mouth, or fingers.

*Douching or washing right after sex will kill HIV.*
It takes only a second for HIV to enter the bloodstream. By the time you would be able to wash the semen away, it would be too late.

*The pill or spermicidal foam kills HIV.*
The pill and spermicides like foams and those found on contraceptive sponges work by killing sperm. But killing sperm does not kill the AIDS virus. Using the pill or any other kind of birth control other than a latex condom will prevent pregnancy, but it won't protect you against HIV.

*Unprotected anal sex is okay for women.*
A lot of women think anal sex is okay because they won't get pregnant. But the lining of the rectum rips easily during anal sex, and HIV can then pass into your bloodstream. The man whose penis is being inserted into the rectum can also be infected if there are cuts or sores on his penis. This also applies to anal sex between two men.

*You can't get HIV the first time you have sex.*
This is the same thing some people think about getting pregnant. It takes only one sexual encounter to get pregnant, and it takes only one sexual encounter to become infected with HIV. It doesn't matter if it's your first time or your fiftieth.

*You can always tell when someone has HIV or AIDS.*
Unless a person is in the last stages of HIV disease, there are usually no outward signs that she or he is infected. The thin people with sores that are often shown on television and that most people associate with AIDS are people who are in advanced stages of the disease. Most people living with HIV look just like you and your friends, and you would never know they were sick unless they told you.

*Ramona Smith*

# A MOTHER'S STORY

*Ramona Smith is on a mission, she says, "to go out and get people to accept people living with HIV as people." A forty-four-year-old mother of three, she is one of the hundreds of thousands of women infected with HIV. Ramona was told she was HIV-positive in 1991. Now she is an AIDS educator with the Urban League and a member of the Virginia Department of Health Minority AIDS Task Force and the HIV Prevention Community Planning Committee.*

*Listening to her as she told her story, I could feel the peace that Ramona has worked so hard to achieve in her life. Reading her words, I hope you will hear it too.*

**How did you respond to the news that you are HIV-positive?**

After getting over the emotional roller coaster of wondering why this happened to me and not knowing what to do, I decided to educate myself so that I could educate others. I began to do a lot of reading. I began to go anyplace I could where I could get information about HIV. And once I felt comfortable that I knew enough about it and felt better about myself, I decided that it was time to go out and educate others.

Unfortunately, this society has an extremely negative view of people with HIV. Many people living with it don't want to deal with the fear and rejection of being isolated or ostracized, so they suffer in silence. I do this because I want people to see that HIV is no respecter of persons. If you have ever been sexually active or ever used needles to inject drugs, then you could have been exposed to it.

There are so many things that I could say about how society has reacted to individuals with this virus, but one point that I would definitely like to make is this: We are supposed to love our neighbors, but so often people turn away from people when they learn that they have the virus. People have got to be educated so that they understand what HIV is and so that they can begin to respond to people living with HIV with compassion and love, not fear and judgment.

**Was it hard to tell your children about your status?**
Making the decision to reveal my medical status to

my children was one that I worried over for a long time. I was able to accept being HIV-positive for myself, and as a mother I felt that I should share my HIV status with my children. But because of all of the negative views and feelings attached to being HIV-positive, I didn't know how to approach my children and share it with them. But once I did, it was extremely easy. I was surprised at how relieving it was to tell them.

**How long did you wait to tell your children?**
I told them about a year after I found out. I kept debating it in my mind. When I told my oldest son, his reaction was exactly what I thought it would be. He wanted to give up his life for my life. He was going to college in New York and he had a good job. He wanted to quit his job and school and come here to take care of me. And that's just what I didn't want. I had to convince him that even though I had HIV, I was still going to school and I was still doing what I wanted to do in life. I would not have been able to go on with my own life if I knew that I had prevented him from doing the same thing. Eventually, after crying and feeling hurt, he came to understand my point of view. But it was hard for him because he wanted to reach out and protect me.

**Were you afraid of what other people would say to your children?**

That was my major concern. I was not afraid of what my children would think of me, because we are very close. My major concern was the major concern of a mother: I was worried about my children and how they would be affected by finding out and by others finding out. Just the other day I was speaking to my middle son, who is twenty-three, and we were talking about how hard it is for him even though I've been living with this virus for more than three years now. He was saying how thankful he is that we are able to talk about it and that I've been able to educate him. And I was especially pleased to hear him say that, to see that by discussing what I have gone through, it has taught him that he must be sexually responsible and protect himself. I think that's great.

**Your daughter was very young when you found out. How did she react?**
She was thirteen when I found out. My concern for her was that, at thirteen, she was at an age when young people are trying to sort through all kinds of things. So my concern for her was that by me being so open about my status, it might be hard for her to accept. But she's taken it very well. And I'm so thankful for all of these things, for the support I get from my family. Because that is something that a lot of people living with this virus never get. We need positive feelings around us. All of us, every human being, want love, especially the love and acceptance of our

families. So if you don't get that, it can be very hard. I've found that often families are afraid because they don't know anything about HIV. Or sometimes they know but they will still treat the family member with the virus in a standoffish way.

**Were your children afraid for you?**
We've talked about how they felt when I told them. But I feel as a mother that even though they've expressed how they felt then and how they feel now, I can never know just what it felt like when it hit them that first time. I don't believe they could actually voice how it felt, just as I can't voice exactly how it felt when my doctor said to me, "Yes, Mrs. Smith, you are infected with HIV." There are moments in life that you can never explain, moments when you can't even comprehend what is going on. And I think that being told you have HIV or being told that someone you love has HIV are definitely some of those moments.

**Has being HIV-positive changed the way you see your children?**
It's made me have a stronger sense of attachment with my children. The way this virus works, you can be fine one day and down the next. So I want to let my children know every day how much I love them and that I will be here for them for as long as I can. I don't want to wait until I'm dying to express my feelings to them. There's nothing sadder than when someone

dies without letting the people around know how much they meant.

**Did you know anything about HIV or AIDS when you were tested?**
I had very little knowledge about HIV. The only thing I knew about HIV was that it was a white, gay, male disease. So I said to myself, "You're not a white, gay man and you're not dating a white, gay man, so you don't have to ever worry about HIV." But the man that I had been engaged to was an ex–IV drug user. One day someone from the department of health came to the house looking for him, but we were no longer living together. This man told me that he was looking for him because he might have a sexually transmitted disease, and his sexual partners needed to see a doctor.

The next day, I went down to the department of health. I sat there in the waiting room looking at all of these signs about HIV and AIDS. I still thought it was a white, gay man's disease, so I had no reason at all to suspect that was why I was down there. So I had the test, and two weeks later I got the results and found out I was positive.

**What did you think then?**
Sometimes we know something but we believe that if we don't think about it and don't talk about it, it will go away. That's how I reacted to finding out. I was

already registered at a university to complete my degree, so when the fall came I just went to school and devoted all of my time and energy to being a college student. I did not think about my medical status at all. But different people were coming to the school and doing HIV and AIDS workshops and whatnot, and something clicked inside me that it was time to wake up to the fact that I was living with this virus.

So I began to educate myself, and I graduated with honors with a degree in interdisciplinary studies. So speaking from an educator's point of view, I feel it is important for me to be able to educate others about this disease along with educating myself. And with AIDS, new material is constantly coming out, and it is so important to keep track of all of the newest findings. So I'm glad that I learned how to educate myself.

**What kinds of activities are you involved in?**
There are a lot of things that I do and that I am involved in regarding AIDS, because I think it is very important for society to learn that it's not who you are but what you do that puts you at risk for contracting HIV. Another thing that I do is to try and help other people living with HIV to get into the same situation that I am in, where they are comfortable enough with their medical situations and with themselves that they can begin to stand up and speak out so that people can see that there are many differ-

ent faces to AIDS, that it's not just one group that is being affected. It's all across the board in every population. There's a lot that needs to be done, and it will get done. It will take a while, but we'll do it. A lot of times when someone dies from AIDS, we say that they died from cancer or something else. We cannot be ashamed to say that someone died from AIDS. We cannot hide it.

**Were you angry at the man who infected you?**
I honestly did not harbor any anger toward him. I think because of my strong belief in God, I was able to accept it and deal with it. When we were together, he was hospitalized for problems with his liver. He never told me that he was HIV-positive, and I don't know that he even knew. I would like to think, for my own peace of mind, that when that man from the department of health came to my house looking for this man, it would have been the first time he knew of his HIV status. But I will never know, because he died before I could ever speak to him about it.

**Do you think it's important for everyone to get tested?**
A lot of people say that they don't want to get tested because they don't want to know if they have this virus. But by not getting tested, they are allowing this virus to spread. If someone is infected and doesn't know it, he can infect his partners. Then if they sleep

with other people, those people get infected. And it just goes on and on and on until that one person has caused a hundred people to get infected as well. But if that first man had found out and had begun immediately to take precautions against infecting his partner, then ninety-nine lives would have been saved. AIDS is a chain reaction. Once one person gets it, it passes on to person after person unless it's stopped. It's like the old African proverb that says that he who conceals his disease cannot be cured.

**Does speaking help you to deal with your feelings about being HIV-positive?**
I am so thankful that I am able to speak out in such a public way about such a private part of my life. Society wants to isolate individuals with HIV and AIDS, and that's why I want to be so open about it.

Whoever opens the door to me, I go in to them and speak. I speak to schools. I speak to churches. I speak to youth. I speak to colleges. I speak to anybody and everybody, because I feel that this story needs to be told. I also feel that you can talk as much as you want about HIV and AIDS, but when you have the chance to talk to someone who actually is living with this virus, then you begin to realize the reality of AIDS.

To look at me, you would never believe that I have this virus. People think that you can look at someone and tell that they have HIV. But honey, there is no way that you can tell. I look just like anyone else's mother, and I have it. That's why I speak, and that's why I tell people to go get tested. HIV can be prevented. But if we keep silent about it, or make people living with the virus feel that they are less than human, then we let it spread.

I feel that each time I do a presentation or a workshop or I speak to a group of people about my experience, I gain another degree of freedom. Because I don't walk around worrying about who knows and who doesn't and I don't have to carry this burden alone. Society does not let people with HIV feel comfortable about being infected, so people who have it walk around in silence, carrying this burden all by themselves.

I truly enjoy being able to encourage people. On my job, I am a case manager for people with HIV. And I always tell them, "There are things that you can't do. But there are things that you can do. So do those things as long as you can." So many of the people that I see have been turned away by their friends or turned away by their families. I thank God that I can hug them and let them know that they aren't alone.

**Do you think about dying?**
I know that a lot of people view HIV as deadly and think death is the worst thing they can face. But I know because of my faith that this isn't my real home

anyway. I'm just passing through here on my way to God's country. Death is my reward anyway, and when it's my time to go, it will be God calling me to him. Not because the virus says it's time to go, but because God says it is. There are days that I do feel down and depressed, and there is not a moment when I don't think about HIV, but I know that there is a reason for it.

I told my daughter, and I told everyone, that I see myself being here for a long, long time. I don't see myself going anywhere anytime soon. I just did a television show, and the young lady on before me said that because she was HIV-positive, she felt like she couldn't make any long-term plans. When I went on, I said that there was one major difference between me and that young lady. And everyone thought I was going to say that she was white and I'm black. But what I said was that I could make plans for five, ten, or fifteen years from now. Because I believe that you need a positive state of mind to deal with this.

**How do you feel about people who say that AIDS is God's punishment on people who do wrong things?** The population that I enjoy speaking to the most is the Christian population, because I think they need to hear the message the most. And my response to people who say that this is God's punishment on people is to say that those of us who profess to be

Christians, who say we follow the teachings of Jesus Christ, know that this is not God's wrath against anybody for sinning. This is a disease. It is our opportunity to look in the mirror and examine ourselves and see how we are measuring up to what Jesus wants of us.

I liken the present-day tragedy of AIDS to the ancient one of leprosy. How did Jesus respond to people with leprosy? He did not respond to them with rejection and fear; he responded to them with love and compassion. Therefore, if I am a Christian, I should not run in fear from a person with AIDS. God is not the author of fear. If I say I am a Christian, but yet I'm doing exactly the opposite of what Jesus did, then I have to look in the mirror and find out why I am acting with fear and judgment instead of with love.

Whenever I close a presentation, I always say, "Remember, someone Jesus loves has AIDS, because Jesus loves us all." Everybody needs love. My message to anyone in regard to this crisis is to reach out with love. I may not understand exactly what you're going through. I may not agree with all of your actions and your ways. But if I respond to you with love, then I truly believe that that love will trigger something inside us both. We may have different points of view, but we have that common bond. United we stand, and divided we fall. And that's how I feel about that.

**Do you ever get angry at God?**
There was a time when I used to sit and wonder why this happened to me, what I did to deserve it and all of that. Then this young lady at church said something to me. She said, "Ramona, God knows your heart. He knew what you would do with being HIV-positive. Look at how you educated yourself and how you educate others." And that helped me see the reason for all of this, and I was so thankful for being able to do what I do.

**Do you feel that God has taken anything away from you?**
I have heard people say that; I sure have. And when I hear them say that, I try to encourage them, to let them know that they still have so much. I've found that people who have some connection to God, or to some form of a higher power, whatever it is, have strength to go on. It's the ones who have nothing to believe in who think only of death. That's all they see. We're all going to die sooner or later, so why worry about crossing the bridge until you get to the bridge? Why sit around waiting to die? You have to go for it and make every moment count. Educate people. Motivate people. It's like I always say, I may not be able to do the things I used to do, but thank God I can do the things that I can do. And it's up to me to go forth and do those things.

**What needs to be done to reach people?**
People don't want to talk about sex. But we must begin to face reality. Because if you educate someone, you put them in a better position to deal with a situation if they get into it. If I never educate my daughter about sex, then she may find herself in a compromising situation and not know how to get out of it. But if, through education, I give her the tools she needs to know that it's her body and that she's a lovable person and doesn't have to have sex to get love, then she will be able to deal with those situations.

My main message is abstinence. But we have to face reality. Young girls are still getting pregnant. And unless they came up with a new way to do it and nobody told me, then young boys are still the ones getting them pregnant. Therefore, let them know that there are alternatives, and that means condoms. Now, condoms are said to be ninety-nine percent safe. But my own personal opinion is, I don't want to be ninety-nine percent safe. I want to be one hundred percent safe. And the only way to do that is no sex. But we know that this society is growing, so somebody is having sex. So just give the people information.

My telling you that a condom provides a barrier between yourself and an infected person is not the same as saying it's okay for you to go out there and have sex. It's giving you information. What you do with that information is up to you.

**How does it make you feel to see your children growing up in a world with AIDS?**
I think it is very sad. I think it's depressing. Years ago, before you got married, you had to have a blood test so that you knew if either of you had anything. Now they don't do that. If I were a young person, I would have the longest engagement in the world. To me, we are living in dark times, because something like making love, something that God meant to be so special, society has taken and devalued. I think we need to go back and educate people to respect themselves and to respect each other. If people began to respect themselves and respect others, then this virus would never get passed to another person. Because when you respect yourself and you respect others, you want to protect them.

**Do you think we will learn anything from the AIDS crisis?**
I really truly don't know. But I am praying that it will help people wake up and realize that you just can't go out there and be sexually active with that one and that one and that one. The virus has your name on it if you're out there participating in the behaviors that put you at risk. My daughter is sixteen, and we talk about her getting married and having children. And you know what she told me? She said, "Ma, at this point I do not want to get married, and I don't want to have children. If I thought about getting married,

the young man I marry would have to have a blood test every other day." It's hard for people her age, because the media sells sex. Sex promotes everything. But nowhere do they teach respect. We need to get back to that.

**What is the most important thing for people to know about AIDS?**
I remember there was a time when people would talk about AIDS and refer to "those people," meaning gays. Now when they say "those people," they mean me and everyone else living with HIV. We need to begin to wake up and look at that. I think it's terrible that when someone says that she or he is HIV-positive, the first question is always, "How did you get it?" It does not matter how an individual got it. The point is that the person has it, and I need to see how I can help.

I believe that there is good in everything. You might have to look long and hard to find it in a lot of situations or in a lot of individuals. But it is there. And if you hold on, and if you have love as your motivator, you will hold on and you will see that good. Once you see that good, you can draw on it and extend it. But if you only dwell on the bad, then you're going to hurt people and chop them down. And that's not what life is about. Life is beautiful, if we allow it to be.

## Condom Sense

Apart from not having sex at all, the best protection against HIV is for a man to wear a latex condom on his penis during anal, oral, or vaginal sex. While condoms do sometimes break, they have been found to be approximately ninety-nine percent effective in preventing the transmission of HIV when used properly. Using a condom properly means:

- never using a condom more than once

- using only latex rubber condoms. Some condoms, usually called skins, are made out of animal membranes and will not prevent the transmission of HIV. Also avoid using condoms that fit over only the tip of the penis, as these do not work.

- lubricating the condom with a water-based lubricant like K-Y jelly and not with oil-based lubricants like

Vaseline or Crisco. Oil-based lubricants can cause a rubber to tear. Many condoms are now lubricated, so this should not be a problem.

- making sure you know how to put a condom on properly: (1) Leave space at the tip for semen to collect in and (2) remove air bubbles from the tip; (3) push all air bubbles out of the rubber by running your fingers down the sides of your penis once the rubber has been rolled on. If you don't know how to do it, practice before you have sex.

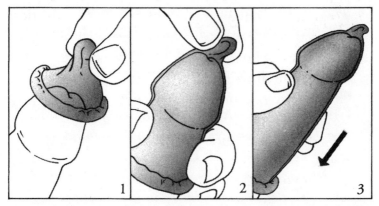

- not storing condoms in your wallet or a car's glove compartment, where they will dry out and possibly break

- using a condom every time you have sex. Yes, it can be a real pain to have to pull one out, open it, and put it on. But it could save your life or the life of your partner.

*John Carlin*

# MAKING MUSIC WITH A MESSAGE

*John Carlin believes that music can make a dif-
ference in the fight against AIDS. In 1989,
frustrated by what they saw as the failure of
AIDS organizations to reach young people with a
message of AIDS awareness and education,
Carlin and his partner, Leigh Blake, formed the
Red Hot Organization. Dedicated to providing
young people with AIDS information, Red Hot
raises money for AIDS organizations by asking
artists in the music industry to lend their voices
to recording projects, videos, and television shows.*

*Red Hot's first release was 1990's Red Hot +
Blue, a collection of classic Cole Porter songs per-
formed by popular artists including k.d. lang,
Sinead O'Connor, the Neville Brothers, David
Byrne, and Neneh Cherry. This was followed by
Red Hot + Dance (1992), a collection of dance
music by artists including George Michael*

*and EMF, and* No Alternative *(1993), an alternative-music album featuring music by Nirvana, Smashing Pumpkins, The Breeders, and Soundgarden, among others. In 1994, the organization produced* Red Hot + Country, *with country stars like Mary Chapin Carpenter, Billy Ray Cyrus, Kathy Mattea, and Dolly Parton; and* Red Hot + Cool, *a hip-hop and jazz collection with offerings from Digable Planets, Herbie Hancock, and Branford Marsalis.*

*In only a few years, the Red Hot Organization has raised more than $5 million for AIDS awareness and education, all of which has gone back into the communities that buy its records.*

**How did you get involved with raising money through the music industry?**
I got involved through a complement of coincidences that came together to put me into this position. I had been an art critic in the early 1980s, hanging out in New York's East Village. That was a community that was extremely hard hit very early on by the AIDS crisis, and that was something that I was very, very aware of. Two of my closest friends either died during that era or became ill and died later.

I was living in one of the early communities where you would talk to somebody and then three months

later find out that they had died. And I had never had
that experience. I had always been a politically active
person, but this was much different. There's a big
difference between protesting the war in Vietnam or
talking about starvation in Africa and having somebody literally next door to you dying in their twenties. Like so many people, I wanted to know what I
could do about this horrible situation.

**So you channeled your frustration into the Red Hot
Organization?**
For other, personal reasons, in the late 1980s I went
from being an art critic to being an entertainment
lawyer. In that capacity, I had access to knowledge of
the entertainment industry that was more concrete
than what I'd had as someone simply involved in the
arts field. In particular, while I was an entertainment
lawyer, I became aware that certain corporations were
using celebrities to raise money and awareness to fight
AIDS, and they weren't always doing so with the
utmost integrity.

Even beyond that, I felt that when things were
being produced by or from a charity, they often were
not working for the very audience for whom they
needed to work most, namely young people. Because
they were out of it, frankly. It was a charity trying to
produce something, and they would produce something that was stodgy or oriented toward their own
demographics. Or they would do this kind of bogus

market research and then produce these sociological-
ly based materials. Some of which could be very positive. But I perceived a need for projects that were
more focused around popular culture. And that's
always been the bedrock on which the Red Hot
Organization operates, that we are going to produce
materials that get into the popular culture not
because they are benefits or are about certain issues,
but because they are good products. And they go out
there into the world and kids are intrigued and interested by them just like they are by any other hot
record or great video.

**You present AIDS education through the music?**
Right. I think we have been able to put very significant AIDS information into our material. A few
weeks ago I read an article, which I really took offense
to, about how the music industry has been slow to
respond to AIDS because there are so few songs about
the issue. For example, the writer was saying how
even though Bruce Springsteen's hit song "Streets of
Philadelphia" is metaphorically about AIDS, he never
comes out and says it's about AIDS. And it was
annoying to me that he chose to ignore the fact that
on our very first record in 1990 there was a song by
Neneh Cherry that was a rap song that told people
what AIDS stands for and what HIV is. That song
did very well, and the video got a lot of attention on
MTV. And that's what we take the most pride in: get-

ting that material out without any apologies for what it is.

**Someone like Neneh Cherry, who is a name in the rap community, is someone young people will listen to.**
Particularly at that time, and so the song had great street credibility and kids listened to it who might not listen to someone else talking about AIDS.

**Tell me a little bit about the first album, *Red Hot + Blue*. How did you come up with that idea?**
Well, what we did was use Cole Porter as a kind of Trojan horse. We picked this very conservative figure who in fact wasn't very conservative when you scratched the surface. He was a gay artist whose work touched upon those themes in very clever and hidden ways because of the culture he operated in. And one of the things that we did that was most interesting was to bring out the subtexts of his songs and show how they could be applied to the issues surrounding AIDS. That way, we were able to get across a positive message about dealing with AIDS without hitting people over the head with it.

**Why did you pick popular music as a way to reach young people?**
When we started this, it was with the sense that young people's lifestyles, the tribal signs that they

associate themselves with, come from popular culture, particularly pop music. Kids dress and behave like rock stars. So the idea is that if you want to get kids to think of condoms as an everyday part of life, fifty-year-old doctors in white suits telling them what to do is going to promote a negative reaction. But Bono, Neneh Cherry, George Michael, or Madonna talking about it is going to have a much different effect. If Bono is not ashamed to talk about this or deal with it, then it changes the issue for young people.

**Do you think the music can actually make a difference?**
I'm totally optimistic. I realize that this is a long, complicated fight, and that a couple of pop songs or appearances on MTV aren't going to change a whole generation. That's in fact why we continue to do these projects. You can't put out a few songs and say, "Okay, I did my bit. See you later." This is something that needs to be repeated all the time, that needs to go out in many, many different genres of music so that it's always in people's faces.

**You've been very successful at choosing types of music that are popular at the moment.**
I just really love music, and I always have. There's nothing better I can imagine doing with my life than making pop culture with a conscience. I love the

music, and I love being involved with it in terms of what's fresh and current. And I love the fact that rather than doing it in what can often be a very sleazy music business, I can do it in a very positive way.

**Are the artists you work with equally enthusiastic?**
It's been an extraordinary experience working with virtually all these artists, and it has completely reconfirmed my respect for artists in general. You know, the people who have shown up for our projects and done them have really been informed and really wanted to do it. A lot of the negative backlash I heard when I started these projects was that stars would only do it because their managers told them to do it or to further their careers, as a good marketing decision or a career pick-me-up. That's not what I found to be true. I've found that people are really genuinely affected by this issue and want to do something about it. And the reason we remain successful is because people, including music stars, are looking for a vehicle, a megaphone to amplify what they wanted to say about this issue. And we have been able to create a platform for them to do that.

**And they all donate their time?**
Yes, this is all done on a strictly volunteer basis.

**How is the money raised by the projects used?**
We distributed over $4 million from the first album,

which is the only one for which we have final numbers. And the way we've distributed the proceeds
from that project is to sprinkle the money in a very
broad way by giving to over a hundred different organizations in thirty different countries around the
world. Sometimes we've given money in large
chunks—like we gave a big chunk to the American
Foundation for AIDS Research to help print a treatment directory. We've given large amounts of money
to activist groups in the United States.

In foreign areas, we've given money to umbrella
organizations and let them make the determination
of where the money could best be used in those areas.
We give the money away in direct proportion to the
record's sales in any given area. So the thought is that
if you buy a copy of the record in Germany, the profits from that sale will go to fund an AIDS organization in Germany.

In the United Kingdom and the United States,
which are our two largest markets, we've given the
money away through a peer-review process where we
sent out a request for proposals with the mandate that
what the Red Hot Organization does is primarily prevention education. Then we set up a panel of experts
who graded the proposals and gave away relatively
small grants of $25,000 to $50,000.

**So theoretically, any AIDS organization could apply
for funding from the Red Hot Organization?**

What we try to do is focus on specific communities or projects. Like right now, we are doing a jazz/hip-hop project. All the profits from that album will go to grassroots organizations dedicated to fighting AIDS among communities of color. We are doing a country album, and the profits from that will go to suburban and rural education programs.

**What have you learned through your work?**
What we learned was that in one sense it's harder to give the money away than it is to raise it. And that there are two things in the world, and in my mind, that justify our continued existence, which are artistic integrity and charitable integrity. The two things I focus on are that our products are good, because I'm not interested in producing junk, and that our money is given away in the cleanest and most efficient way.

I think the other important point to make is that I really believe that the existence of our product in the world is more significant than the money that we raise, even though the scale of the money has been quite significant. I think it's more important that a young person is sitting there with an album and reading what it has to say and listening to the content of the songs than it is that that album's purchase may have generated four or five dollars in profit.

**What other education efforts are you involved in?**
We do television projects for each record, and those

contain much more information than the records. For example, the *Red Hot + Dance* special had interviews with HIV-positive kids that actually ran as part of the show.

**Are you happy with the success of these efforts?**
You know, it's tough. The shows ran on MTV and VH-1 and won awards, but it's hard to measure their success. You send these things out into the world, and it's very rare that you get response back or someone says, "I saw your show and it changed my life."

**Do you feel like these efforts are working?**
No one show or record or person is going to make a difference. It's the concert of voices of all of the people out there doing this kind of thing in the world that will make a difference. Together we will make a difference. It's a tough one. I mean, look how hard it's been to get kids to stop smoking.

**What kind of message do you think kids are getting from your projects?**
I don't know for sure what they're getting. I hope that the message they're getting is that AIDS is something that you can talk about and is an unfortunate but unavoidable fact of our existence. But in addition to that, that it's not something that their lives need to revolve around or that they have to live in paranoia and dread over. Our message has always been, Have

fun while you're young. Just be smart about it. We definitely are not pushing "just say no," because we know that doesn't work. Kids are going to experiment, and they should be careful. It's like the catch phrase that we used for *Red Hot + Blue:* "romance with intelligence."

**How has being involved with the projects affected you the most?**
That's hard to say. In a spiritual sense, it has certainly enriched my life and given me a tremendous sense of self-worth. In a material sense, it's made my life very difficult, because I gave up a much more economically remunerative job. I had a very successful career in a material sense. This is a real struggle. We never have enough money to do what we want to do, particularly on the scale we are now doing things. So it's been tough. I really think of this as fighting a war, and we're in the middle of this war and I feel real good for fighting in it. But it's painful, and it takes its toll.

**What's next for Red Hot?**
I'm not sure. We've done five projects now, which is a fairly monumental series. Nobody's ever done a series of charitable projects before. I'm going to sit and wait and see how the world responds to that, whether they say, "That's enough; go do something else" or "You've created this great thing; keep going." I guess for my mind I can't tell whether Red Hot is this great pro-

duction company that in four years produced five records and TV shows to fight AIDS or whether it's become a broader charitable organization like a Greenpeace or Amnesty International where young people, when they want to do something about AIDS, look at us as a focus point.

**Is that what you'd like to be—an organization for youth interested in getting involved in the fight against AIDS?**
Something like that needs to exist. It's not that I want to create another AIDS organization; I think there are enough of them in the world. But I do think that nobody from within that world has ever created something that kids really respond to. I don't want to create a new institution; that's the last thing on my mind. What I'm saying is that if Red Hot is essentially a mark that means something in the world and has significance to people, and I get enough of a response to that, I'll do everything I can to use that mark in the most valuable, positive way.

**How else would you try to reach young people?**
We have done things other than records and TV shows. For example, we did a series of safer-sex posters and postcards. Now we are thinking about doing one centered around drug use. And we're trying to find ways to distribute condoms to kids. You know, just ways to break the ice and get kids to talk

about sex. We want to explore ways that are out of the mainstream, and explore different ways to reach kids than the ways that have already been tried.

**What keeps you going when it gets hard?**
I would have given this up a long time ago if it were a commercial business. But it's very sustaining to be given the opportunity to do something so positive in the world. Very few people get to measure themselves by what they do and not who they are, and I consider that to be a tremendous fortune in my life. Even though Red Hot is something I created, I really see it as something that was entrusted to me. My role is to guide it. I have been given this thing that has more value, is so significantly larger than myself. It's not something that is about self-expression; it's a social tool.

# Talking about Safer Sex

Talking with your girlfriend or boyfriend about safer sex can be hard to do. It can even be embarrassing. After all, it's often a lot easier to have sex than it is to talk about it! But AIDS is something you can't afford not to talk about, and there are ways to bring the subject up and make it easier for both of you.

You can try giving your partner a book like this one, or starting a conversation about some kind of AIDS topic. You might mention something you saw on a talk show or in a movie, or you could get some safer-sex information from an AIDS organization and share it with your partner. A lot of AIDS organizations also offer safer-sex workshops that you can attend by yourself or with your partner.

Your greatest weapon in fighting AIDS is respecting yourself and respecting others. If you respect yourself, then you are not going to put yourself at risk for contracting HIV and you are not going to let anyone else put you at risk. And if you respect others, you will want to protect them from infection as well.

You are an important person. While you may feel down sometimes, think that it doesn't matter whether you get HIV or not, or think that no one cares, you should always try to remember that you are worth taking care of. Don't let someone talk you into doing something you don't really want to do just because you think it will make them like you or love you. Anyone who says he loves you just because you have sex with him, or who says she loves you just because you use drugs with her, isn't worth loving. Don't waste your time on someone who doesn't respect you for what you are or someone who wants to put you at risk because he or she is too selfish to use condoms.

It can be very hard to ask someone to use a condom, or to refuse to have sex with someone who won't. That person may even try to make you feel stupid, like you're somehow a loser or a wimp for being strong enough to protect yourself. But no one is more important than you are, and no one is worth losing your self-respect for. If you can remember that, then you won't let yourself get into potentially harmful situations.

# *Antigone Hodgins*

## LEADING THE FIGHT

*In 1987, when nineteen-year-old Antigone Hodgins asked her family doctor to test her for HIV, he refused, saying that he could tell that she did not have the virus. Confident that she was not infected, she did not push for the test. Three years later Antigone was tested, and the results came back positive. She believes she was infected when she was sixteen.*

*One of the first places Antigone went after she learned of her HIV status was Bay Area Young Positives, a group in San Francisco that offers support to young people dealing with HIV and AIDS. Now she is the executive director of B.A.Y. Positives, using her experiences to help other young people. One of the few young people heading a major AIDS organization, Antigone believes that as the AIDS crisis moves into its second decade, it is more important than ever for teenagers to become involved in the fight against the disease that is claiming more and more young lives every year.*

**What did you know about HIV when you were a teenager?**
I started seeing a lot of billboards about condoms. These weren't aimed at any specific groups, so in the back of my mind was this thought that there was this teeny tiny chance that I could get HIV. But I didn't really take it seriously because when I was in school we never talked about HIV or AIDS or anything. The only time we ever talked about it was once in home-room when the teacher said that HIV was in blood, semen, vaginal secretions, and saliva. He said that it was found in saliva; that's how little we knew about it. Then someone made a homophobic joke and everyone laughed, and that was it. Even the teacher laughed. So that's why I didn't feel at risk.

**What made you get tested?**
When I was nineteen, I went to the doctor I was see-ing and I asked him about getting tested for HIV. His response was, "I can tell by looking at you that there's a ninety-nine percent chance that you're negative." He said that if I really wanted to get tested, I could go to an anonymous test site. I had no idea what he was talking about, and the idea of calling someplace to find out how to get tested was unreal to me. Here's

this doctor, who's supposed to know better, standing there telling me he could tell by looking at me that I was okay. And also at that time, all you ever saw about AIDS was pictures of skinny men who were sick. I never saw pictures of people who were healthy-looking. So I really thought he was right.

So I waited until I was twenty-two to get tested. And the reason I finally did it then was because I stopped drinking when I was twenty and I was making a lot of changes in my life—health and lifestyle changes. A friend of mine, an older gay man, was going to get tested, and I asked if I could go too. So he made an appointment at an anonymous test site, and we went.

**Did you ever think that you'd be positive?**
I figured there was a fifty-fifty chance, that either I was or I wasn't. But no, I really didn't think I would be. When I went for the results, my mother came with me. I went in, and this counselor took me to this room. We sat down and she asked me if I had any questions. At that point I just wanted the results, so of course I didn't have any questions. Then she tells me that I'm positive.

**How did you react?**
I immediately was just so scared and completely shocked. All I could say was, "Oh my God." I started crying. I immediately felt like I was bad, because I

had a lot of shame about my behavior when I was drinking. And all that came up again. Every bad thing I'd ever heard people say about people with HIV went through my head, like "What did you do to get it?" and "She deserved it because she was promiscuous." All this stuff. All I could say to this counselor was, "Can you go get my mother?"

I think the counselor didn't know what to do because she had no idea a young woman would be coming in that day, because I wasn't the typical person that would go there for testing. And she was a young woman as well, and I think it was all too close to home. She kept asking me questions, and all I could say was, "Please go get my mother. She's sitting outside in the car. Please go get her." My mother was sitting parked in a bus zone waiting for me, because since I assumed I would be negative, we thought it would be this in-and-out thing. So my mom came in, and we just sat there and cried.

**How did you deal with it?**
The first few months, I had a really hard time telling anybody. I was in college, and I was taking classes. I told a couple of professors, but that was it. I was going back to school to become a therapist. That's what I wanted to go into, the helping field. But it was so hard for me to go to school, to take the bus even and be around people my age. Because I just felt so isolated. I felt like I was so alone and no one would

understand what I was going through. I'd go into the bathroom, and women talk to each other a lot in the bathroom. I'd overhear these conversations, and they'd be talking about things so far in the future, as if they had seventy years left. And I was thinking that I had six months. I really believed that. I was filled with fear, and I just felt like I couldn't be around that kind of thing. So I was going to school less and less and was just really depressed.

Basically, all I could do for six months was play video games. I was living at home with my mom, and I would sit for hours trying to get to the next level of Super Mario Brothers. That game literally saved my life. It was really symbolic for me, like if I could get through the next level, I could stay alive. I needed something like that because every morning I woke up and my first thought was that I was going to die. At night I couldn't sleep. I slept with my mom for the first few months, and I had her read *Winnie the Pooh* to me and we'd look at the pictures. It was like I was trying to be a child again because that felt safe.

**What did your dad do?**
My dad had a hard time with it. He has a hard time with death, so whenever I would call and talk about dying, he'd get all upset and tell me not to talk about it. His big thing was taking action—getting onto an insurance plan, getting a doctor, finding books. His response is typical, I think, of a lot of fathers who find

out, which is "Let's take care of this problem and everything will be all right, so stop crying." He's gotten a lot better, but for a long time he couldn't even talk about it.

**How did you educate yourself once you found out you were positive?**
The day I found out, I had an appointment with my therapist, which I'd set up just in case I was positive. So I had that. There was also a library right down the street from my house, and I went to the library. That was hard, because I felt like telling everyone I saw that I had HIV, but I couldn't. I started looking for books, and there was just nothing there. And when it came to AIDS and women, forget it. So I went to a bookstore and bought a whole bunch of books on the subject.

I actually knew quite a bit about HIV. I knew how you could and couldn't get it and all of that. I'd just never thought about that knowledge in relation to myself, because I never thought that I would need to. But I didn't know about more technical things, like T-cells and things, so I needed to educate myself about that. It really helped to read.

I also went to B.A.Y. Positives three days after I tested and joined a support group. Throughout those first three months I was going to the group, and I was able to meet other people living with HIV. And that just helped so much. I feel that I never would have been able to do all of the work I've done if I hadn't had that initial support from the group here. At the time, the group was mainly young gay men, except for one other woman and myself. But I was still able to identify with them because we were all young people, and that's what I needed, other young people to talk to about HIV. They really took me in, and I felt like I was walking into a family. It was like I walked toward them and into their arms, and they held me. The first night I was there, I was crying the whole time, and everyone was really supportive.

After that, I dropped out of college because I just couldn't deal with it all. Besides, I figured a degree would be useless if I was dead. I did peer education for a while, but I never disclosed my HIV status to anyone, including the other people I was working with. Then I started to speak in high schools, and I came out about my HIV status. That started the whole thing. Suddenly I was on all of these committees and working all of the time.

**You really threw yourself into it.**
I sure did. At the time, I was one of the only young women out about being HIV-positive, so everyone wanted me to speak. I felt like I needed to do it, because I felt like I was proving to myself that I wasn't dying.

**Did you ever think you'd be doing anything like this?**

No way; not at all. Before I got involved in HIV/AIDS education, I had worked in a movie theater and in a bookstore. When I was working at the movie theater, we would have these conversations about AIDS. I always said that if I ever found out I was positive, I would just take a big fat shot of dope and kill myself. Then when it happened, it was like an invisible thread started pulling me to all these different support groups, and I just started going. I hit the ground and started running.

I guess I went for things that made me feel good. Like when I spoke, people would come up to me and say, "You're so brave," and that really helped me a lot. My self-esteem was really minuscule. No one ever listened to me in my family life. I'd be at the dinner table and I'd have to ask three times for someone to pass the potatoes. And here I was speaking, and people were on the edges of their seats. I realized how much power I had, and I really took to public speaking. I used to never be able to talk in front of people in high school. But by doing this, I learned to talk.

**How did your friends react to you when they found out?**

They were pretty much just really shocked. Some of them went and got tested, because they figured that if I could be infected, then they could too. A lot of them just did not know how to deal with me. They knew they could be around me, because they knew enough about it that they knew they couldn't get the virus from casual contact. So that was not the issue. What was more the issue was that here I was, twenty-two years old, and they had no idea what to say to me. Also, I had needs that they couldn't meet. They didn't know what I wanted, and I wasn't even sure what I wanted from them. It was really hard. Most of my friends started to become other young people with HIV. Only now, after four years, am I able to go back and have my old friends again.

There was also, for me, a lot of jealousy. Even now. I'm going to be in my friend's wedding soon, and that will be hard. Before I had HIV, I never wanted to get married; I never wanted kids. Now that I can't have that stuff, it makes me angry when I realize that I can't have the things my friends are having. And my friends didn't realize that when they talked about those things, it really affected me.

**Is it hard to accept that you can't have children?**
The decision that I've come to is, I can have kids if I want to. I have that right, and I'm not going to let society tell me I can't. Because the transmission rate to unborn children can be controlled to some degree. And I feel like I have regained some control over that area of my life because I can make an informed decision if I ever decide that

I might want children. So that's a lot better now.

**How does being positive affect your attitude in terms of romantic relationships?**
In the beginning, I felt completely nonsexual. I really thought that I would never be sexually active again, because I thought that no one would ever want me. Then, about three months after I joined my support group, I met a young man who was positive. We started dating, and that was really helpful for me. In the beginning, I thought that the only kind of person I could ever date was someone else who had HIV. So dating him was really normal. I could be sexually active, and he would come over and we'd watch videos and my mom was all excited because everything seemed normal again. That lasted about three months, because I came to realize that both of you having HIV is just not enough. You still have to have all of the same things you'd have in any relationship, like being compatible personalitywise. But it did a lot to make me feel normal again, and since then I've dated both HIV-positive and HIV-negative people.

**How hard is it to talk to potential partners about your HIV status?**
I tell them almost immediately. I try not to, because I want them to get to know me first, but I always end up doing it. I've never had anyone reject me right up front. It seems like I'm more freaked out about it than

they are. I was celibate for about a year after I tested, and that was really good for me. Like a lot of young people, I had been very sexually active, and taking a break from that really helped me work on my self-esteem and realize that I didn't need sex to be happy.

**Is the romantic issue a big issue with young people who are HIV-positive?**
I've met hundreds of young people with HIV now, and it's an issue with every one of them. It's a huge issue before they find out, and it's an even bigger one after they find out. People put themselves at risk for HIV for reasons. I put myself at risk for a reason. It wasn't like I just decided that I wanted to run out and have lots of sex. There was a hole inside me that I was trying to fill by having sex. This hole wasn't being filled by my family, and I didn't know how to fill it myself. Guys were telling me how much they liked me, and I thought that I had to have sex to keep them liking me. In my mind, they were filling this hole.

When I found out I had HIV, I was scared because I thought I could no longer use sex to fill that empty place inside me. Then I learned more about myself and realized that I didn't need sex to do that. And now I realize that I can have sex for the right reasons and not just to try and build up my self-esteem.

**Were you angry that no one had told you that you could be infected?**

I'm still angry. What got me involved in AIDS education in the first place was my anger. I was so mad.
When I went to the group and I saw that there were
all of these other young people, I was like, "Wait a
minute. I am not alone. Why are all of these young
people infected? There is no reason for us to be infected." And I'm angry that it's still happening, that people still can't talk honestly about sex in schools, that
gay youth and bisexual youth are still almost completely ignored, that sexuality in general is not talked
about. I'm angry that people still resist talking about
safer sex and only want to talk about abstinence.

**With teenagers, and teenage women especially—
among the fastest-growing groups of those infected
with HIV—why do you think we still don't talk
about these issues?**
Why? Because this is America. I don't know if you've
ever seen the AIDS education posters in places like
Sweden and France, but they are much more graphic
than anything we've ever done here. And in those
places where these issues are talked about more openly and condoms have been made readily available, the
rate of HIV infection has gone down dramatically.
But here, where we won't talk about these things, we
still have an increasing infection rate among young
people. Among everyone, but especially among
young people.

Beyond that, we do not even talk about testing for

young people, and I think we've really missed the boat on that. For me, there was always this double message. It was like they were saying I should use condoms, but I didn't need to bother getting tested because I probably didn't have it anyway. What I was hearing was that I didn't need to be tested, so I translated that into the message that I probably wasn't at risk. And that's still happening.

It's all about fear. It's the fear that young people can't handle the responsibility. It's fear of challenging the system. And it's really that people just don't want to know that young people are having sex or getting HIV. The way that HIV is spread most in this country, and probably everywhere, is through people not even knowing their HIV status. They really don't know, so they don't practice safer sex.

**What kinds of problems do women dealing with HIV infection face?**
I think that there is a lot of hostility toward women with HIV and AIDS, especially pregnant women. When a woman is pregnant and HIV-positive, everyone is immediately concerned with what will happen to her fetus. Their concern is not with the woman's health, but with the health of the fetus.

When men, at least straight men, become infected, people feel sorry for them. When women become infected, people assume it's because they did something, and they often say they deserve it.

Another frustrating thing is that I've walked into a lot of support groups for people living with HIV and had people ask me if I'm in the right place because I'm a woman. I've really felt out of place as a woman in the AIDS community.

**Do you think that we will start to blame people who become infected now that more information is available?**
I see that already starting to happen. A lot of the people we see at B.A.Y. Positives are twenty or twenty-one, which means they were probably infected after information should have been available to them to prevent that from happening. But rather than asking how these young people were infected, we need to look at the AIDS prevention messages we are sending young people, because obviously they are not working. The message right now is, if you are heterosexual, use a condom. And that's it. We don't take into account all the other issues, like self-esteem, denial, invisibility of certain groups—all of these things.

I think that the adult population just doesn't understand what young people are going through. I speak a lot in high schools, and I usually go with an older speaker. And a lot of times, the older speakers will tell the kids that they shouldn't think of themselves as invincible. Well, that's normal for young people to think. So we have to work with that attitude and see what we can do about helping them change in other areas of their lives. Risk taking is normal behavior for young people, and you will never stop that. So you have to find other ways to educate them. We have to give young people healthy choices and alternatives and let them choose. You can't just say, "Don't have sex."

**What keeps you going?**
I have really been trying to find a line between work and my private life. Even though a lot of my friends are involved in the AIDS crisis, I've been trying to find more outside interests. But work keeps me going. It's a lot of fun in many ways.

I also hang out with my sister a lot. We're close in age, and she has this whole group of friends around my age. We get together and watch movies all day or whatever, and they don't talk about death or anything related to AIDS. They're just normal, everyday young people. We'll just sit around and watch *Star Trek* or go to bad action movies and have a good time. And they are not involved at all in AIDS, so it helps me escape for a little while.

**How does your sister handle your infection?**
It's really hard on her. I raised her in many ways, and we are close in age. For a long time, she wasn't able to talk about it. It scares her, especially the idea of me dying.

**Do you think about dying?**
I've fallen into a place of denial on that one. I did in
the beginning. I thought about it a lot and read about
it a lot. I have a lot of fear about dying because I was
not brought up with an acceptance of death. But I've
been very healthy, so I don't think about it all that
much now.

I think I was infected when I was sixteen, so sometimes I let myself believe that maybe it was a weaker
virus then and I'll be able to beat it. I do not
have full-blown AIDS, and I've had very few
infections, so I feel fine. I actually feel healthier now
than I've ever felt in my life. I joined a gym. I lost
weight. I look better than I ever have. So I think
about it and I keep on top of things, but I try not to
obsess over it.

**How do you think the AIDS crisis has changed life
in this country the most?**
The AIDS crisis has put a microscope over America
and made people look at all of these issues that have
been hidden for so long: issues around sex, race, class,
age—all of these things. The people in charge have
never wanted to deal with these issues in the first
place, which is why they were hidden. Now we have
to look at them, and that scares people. It's frustrating, but I've seen a lot of changes as well. I've seen
young people with HIV really come to the forefront
of this crisis. We need to have a national committee

of young people with HIV, and that is finally starting to happen.

**Will it be young people who help to end the AIDS crisis?**
I certainly hope so. And not even just young people who are infected. We need to get uninfected young people involved as well. Everyone on our staff is a young person living with HIV. Our whole board of directors is made up of young people. And I think that sends a really powerful message to other young people. They see that we can do it, and they start to believe that they can do it.

# *Eleven*

## Testing: Should I or Shouldn't I?

The only way to find out if you are HIV-positive is to be tested for the presence of the AIDS virus. This can be done with a simple blood test.

There is some debate as to whether people should or should not be tested for HIV. Some people believe that as long as we all assume that everyone is infected and act accordingly, knowing whether we are or are not infected does not matter. Others believe that knowing as soon as possible allows a person to take advantage of the treatments available for people infected with HIV.

The choice to get tested or not get tested is up to you. If you do decide to get tested for HIV, it is important to remember several things:

• Always go to a testing site operated by an established AIDS organization or by your city's department of health. Because there are few rules regarding who can run an HIV testing center or how the tests must be done, you should always check with a local AIDS information organization to see where they recommend going. If you can't find an AIDS organization in your area (look in the yellow pages under AIDS), you can call your local department of health, and they should be able to help you. Most cities also have set up AIDS hot lines to provide information about testing.

• If possible, you should go to a test site that offers *anonymous* testing. This means that they do not ask for your name, address, or any other personal information. You will be assigned a number, and that number will be used to label the blood sample taken from you. When you come back for your results (usually in about two weeks), they will identify you by your number. This is important, because you want your test results to be private information. Test sites that offer *confidential* testing keep records of your test results that include your name. While no one is ever supposed to see these records, mistakes can happen, and you don't want anyone to have information about your HIV status unless you give it to them.

• You can also get tested for HIV in a private doctor's office. If you decide to do this, make sure that the doctor you choose is either someone you know and trust or someone with experience working with AIDS.

- While the presence of the AIDS virus can usually be seen within days or weeks of a person becoming infected, it can sometimes take longer for the virus to be found. If you have participated in risky behavior, it is a good idea to get tested several times, perhaps every six months for a year or two, to make sure of your status. During this time you should not engage in further risky activities, or you won't know for sure if the results of your test are accurate.

- HIV tests *can* be wrong. While it does not happen very often, it is possible to get a false result on an HIV test, either negative or positive. If for some reason you think your results could be wrong, get tested again.

- Just because you test HIV-negative does not mean that you are free to do whatever you want to. You must still be responsible and practice safer sex, as you can still become infected.

- Just because you test HIV-positive does not mean that your life is over, as you can see by the stories in this book. There are thousands of people living with HIV. If you test positive, make sure that you ask for information about finding support groups.

• Most cities have groups specially designed to help people with HIV and answer any questions they might have on issues ranging from available treatments to emotional counseling. They can be located by looking in the yellow pages under AIDS or by calling a local lesbian-and-gay community center, many of which sponsor such groups.

# MY FRIEND

*Krista Blake*

*I first spoke with Krista Blake in 1992, when I was researching my book* 100 Questions & Answers about AIDS. *Krista was twenty years old and had known that she was HIV-positive for a little over a year. She was very angry—at herself, at the boyfriend who had knowingly infected her, at the virus inside of her body. Yet she was also filled with a love of life that came from having to confront her illness head-on. She was determined to defeat her illness with a constant tour of speaking engagements, television appearances, and magazine interviews.*

*Over the next year and a half, Krista called me often. Sometimes she was happy, telling me about her recent date with a marine cadet or a particularly good school appearance. Other times she called me in the middle of the night,*

*depressed and frightened, afraid that she was*
*going to die alone.*

    *Krista died in the spring of 1994 after being*
*in and out of the hospital with various infections.*
*She was twenty-three. I am including the last*
*interview I did with her in memory of all the*
*times she woke me up at two in the morning to*
*tell me she was still going. I miss her.*

**You found out by accident that you were HIV-positive?**
I was having terrible back pains. It hurt so bad that
one morning I was driving my car and I went left
instead of right. If there had been a car coming, I
would have been dead. And that was when
I stopped and said, "I've got to make the doctor
listen to me. I've got to make him find out what's
wrong."

**And when he said he was doing an HIV test, what did you think?**
I said, "You know, I don't think it's really necessary."
He didn't think it was necessary either, but in Ohio
the HIV antibody test was part of the complete diag-
nostic procedure he was doing. We figured we might
as well get it out of the way first.

**So the test results came back and they were positive?**
The first test was inconclusive. They got enough so

that they couldn't say negative but not enough to say it was positive. So they did a DNA test, where they actually look for the virus. They had to call the Centers for Disease Control and get permission to send a DNA sample down.

**What were you thinking while you were waiting for the results?**
During the first test I was anxious and nervous, but it was like having any test done. I told myself, "Wait a minute. You don't have anything to worry about." But then they come back with these questionable results, and now they're sending a sample to the CDC. So I go back and ask this guy I had been with if he was infected and he says no. Then his mother tells me he isn't infected. So I pretty much have this false sense of confidence, because the only guy who could put me at risk said he wasn't infected. Then my results come back and I'm positive.

**And this guy still says it wasn't him?**
Yes. But I know it was him.

**What was your first reaction to this guy?**
I was incensed. I don't even think that word is strong enough. I wanted to kill him. I didn't understand how anybody could do this to somebody else, how they could lie to somebody else about something so important.

**You had no reason to suspect that he was infected when you were involved with him?**
No, because I thought I knew everything about him. After we broke up we were still friends. So it wasn't a stab-in-the-dark kind of thing. He had told me intimate things about his former girlfriends. We really knew a lot about each other, so I didn't think I had anything to worry about, because he had always been so forthcoming with things when I asked questions. I figured that when I asked him if he had AIDS, he would answer me honestly because he had answered everything else so honestly. But he didn't. I asked him before the test and after, and he said no both times.

**But you think he knew all along?**
That I'm not sure. I know that he knew before we started dating, but I don't know how long before that he knew.

**Why do you think he didn't tell you?**
I think he was embarrassed. I think he was afraid that everyone would automatically assume he was gay. I think that he thought people would be different to him. And I don't think he realized, for whatever reason, that women could be infected through sexual contact. I wonder if he even realized he was putting me in danger. I don't think in 1988 we realized that women could be infected sexually. I think we knew that they could be infected from IV drug use and nee-

dle sharing, but I don't know that we knew of the sexual route then.

**You're eighteen years old, six months out of high school, and you find out you're positive for the AIDS virus. Did you know anything about AIDS?**
Not really. They didn't tell me much about HIV in school. The only time we talked about it was in a class about government structure. We talked about it in respect to how much it cost the country. We talked about it in terms of money. So now I have this idea of how much of a burden I'm going to be on society because of what I got out of this government class, and I have to deal with the idea that somebody lied to me and killed me. And that's it; that's all.

**Did you go to a support group?**
Yeah, I tried to go through a support group, but it didn't work. I found that it was a lot of people who wanted to feel sorry for themselves, and I didn't want to feel sorry for myself. I wanted to deal with my feelings and get on with my life. So I got a private counselor. My family is very supportive. And my doctor is my family doctor. He's very good. I can call him if I feel like crap or have questions.

**And did your friends all stay with you?**
Yes. I actually had one girlfriend who moved to Florida right after I was diagnosed, and she felt so

incredibly guilty because she didn't stay with me. I had to say to her, "Please go and live your own life, because what are you going to do when I die? Are you going to be thirty or forty or fifty and not have done what you wanted to do because you felt like you had to be here with me?" I want her to get on with her life, because she's going to be able to do things that I won't be able to do, and I can do them through her.

**Do you feel cheated?**
No, I don't feel cheated, because I still do what I did before. I still go to see my cousins and go to the beach. I spend time with my family. I try to spend time with my friends; I write them and call them. Some people only get twenty or twenty-five years to do everything. Other people have a whole lifetime and they wait around until they're sixty or seventy and then think about all the things they wish they would have done. But I know this might be the end of my life. I go out and spend money like it grows on trees, because that's what it takes to enjoy being alive. Who cares about money when I'm dead? I'm going to spend it while I'm alive and well enough to enjoy it. A lot of people don't like that attitude, but they don't understand.

**What's been the biggest change—?**
You don't even have to finish the question. It's no kids.

**Did you want children?**
I never thought I did, but being told you can't have them is horrible. I guess I realized that a woman for her entire life worries about being pregnant when she doesn't want to be pregnant. But to be able to get pregnant, to be a parent, to choose to carry a child— I don't have these things. I can still physically become pregnant, but I would have to have an abortion because of what the baby would have and what it would do to my body. And I would never put myself in that situation. Obviously I have to use condoms every time I have sex. But still, to have that choice taken away from you is the worst thing.

**When people know you have AIDS, do they automatically think you can't have sex?**
A lot of younger people seem to think that for some reason desire goes away. They think you don't need what other people need or want. But like I tell them, your hormones don't cease to work just because you're HIV-positive. I don't not have desires. That never goes away. Sometimes you wish it did, but it doesn't. You just have to be responsible about dealing with your desires.

**Do you think a lot about dying?**
I think about it. I prepare my affairs and prepare other people and make other people deal with the fact that it's going to happen. But I don't sit around and

think, When am I going to die? How am I going to die? How much longer do I have? I'm not obsessive about it. It's not like I live in constant fear of it. I've accepted it. It will come to me. Some people see that as dwelling on it, and just because I say I'm going to die, they think I'm obsessed. It's not an obsession; it's real. If I sat in my house and didn't go anywhere because I was afraid of getting sick, then I would be obsessed with death. But I still live and still do things and be all I can be. I've made out a will. I made it when I was eighteen years old. But I made out this will and I told everybody what they're getting. And then I said, "Now you've got to outlive me to get it, and I bet I'll win."

**You don't let it hold you back?**
No. Because I'm going to die when I'm going to die and it's not going to matter what I do, because when it's time to die it's time to die. You can't stop it. What if you get hit by a bus? Can you control that? Can you think, Okay, because I might get hit by a bus I'm not going to cross the street? No, you cross the street anyway.

**So what you do hasn't changed?**
It has in the fact that I don't do it as much, I don't do it as late, and I don't do it as fast. It takes me longer to get ready in the morning. It takes me longer to put on my makeup. I don't go out as much, or if I do go

out, I don't stay out as late. I'm home in bed by eleven
on Saturday night. And I can't always do what everybody else is doing. Like I can't always go to the
movies, because I might catch germs from someone.
So I rent videos, which is actually better because you
can get up and make popcorn when you want to and
you can pee when you have to pee.

**Do people who don't know you treat you different-
ly when they find out you have AIDS?**
Sometimes. Some people are cold to me. Some people think it's cool to be my friend, to be friends with
the girl with AIDS.

**What's the biggest misconception about people with
AIDS?**
That we instantly lose a lot of weight and our hair
falls out and we're covered with sores. They think that
everyone with AIDS looks like a person dying in a
hospital. They also think we instantly turn into in-
valids, that we need them to do more for us than they
did for us before they found out. All they need to do
is keep doing the things they always did. Unless we
ask, they just need to be what they've been to us for
as long as they can—friends, mother and father,
grandmother. I need you to be my friend, and part of
you being my friend might be having plans to go out
and then having to change them because I don't feel
good. Maybe we were going to go to dinner. Now I

don't feel good, so why don't you come over and I'll cook for you. Why don't you bring the groceries over, or we'll go out shopping together and cook together. That kind of stuff.

**But don't treat you differently.**
Not unless I ask you to. Obviously, if I ask you for something, I need it. But don't think you have to do it if you didn't do it before. Because all of us realize that there's going to be sometime that we won't be able to do it all, so we want to do what we can while we can.

**What do you want to do in the next ten years?**
I want to swim with sharks. I want to do everything I've ever wanted to. I don't want a job; that would be a ridiculous waste of time for me. I don't want to go to college. I know everything there is to know about what I want to do anyway, so why do that? I have the best education I could ever have—I'm living with a disease. Not dying from it—living with it. That's better than any master's degree or education that you can get at school. AIDS is a great teacher.

**Has AIDS made you grow up more quickly than you would like?**
It has made me accept my goals a lot more quickly. I was pulled out of the game the second that test came back, and I had to decide what was important. I had

to know that immediately. I didn't have two years of college to decide what I wanted to do with my life and then two more years to decide how to do it best. I had to decide now.

**Now you travel and talk to other young people. What's the most important thing to tell young people about AIDS?**
It doesn't matter how much money your mom and dad make, where you live, what your grades are. All that matters is if you make good decisions. One time—that's all it takes.

I don't think it's that kids think that kids can't get AIDS. It's that they think that they're special, so they can't get it. It's like, "I'm so smart that I'm not going to get it, because if I die, it will be a great loss. I have too much to give. But she's on welfare, she isn't as smart, so she'll get it." Well, my question to them is, What makes your life worth living? Why are you lucky and why was I unlucky? Have you really been lucky, or do you just think you are? And how long are you willing to risk your life with luck?

**Is there anything you wish you had known three years ago, before you were infected?**
I wish I had known that that guy was infected. Then I never would have had sex with him. But I don't think that in 1988 scientists knew the things that I would have needed to know. It's not a matter of them

withholding information from me; it was that they didn't have the information that I needed yet. Nobody thought women could get it. At sixteen I knew that gay people got it, that IV drug users got it, and that hemophiliacs got it because they got blood transfusions. But I didn't know about protected sex or unprotected sex. We definitely did not talk about AIDS as a sexually transmitted disease. We definitely didn't cover it in health class. It was something other people got. It wasn't something that was considered pertinent information to give kids. My health teacher didn't even tell us about sex, let alone about sexually transmitted diseases [STDs], so we could never get him to talk about AIDS. And the gym teacher talked about STDs and stuff, but I don't think that for a group of girls AIDS was considered an STD in 1987.

**You didn't know about protected sex?**
I remember we talked about the pill, the IUD, and the diaphragm, but condoms were not the big push. I don't think the teacher pushed anything, but I think all of us left there feeling that if we were going to use birth control, we were going to get on the pill because it was easiest and best. But we were thinking about pregnancy. We weren't concerned with dying.

**Are we doing enough for AIDS education?**
No, and that's because we're always embarrassed about sex. People want their kids to know the facts,

but no one wants to admit that the kids are having sex and doing drugs. We just say, "Don't do it." We don't want our kids to experiment, but that's what kids have to do. They have to explore sexuality, sexual feelings, sexual desires, because that's what makes us all individuals. There's not one thing that's right for an entire group of people. We're allowed to make mistakes, and these people who say God is punishing us for our choices are really sad. If we mess up, God understands that it's because we're human. And we can say, "We were wrong; let's see if we can be right next time."

AIDS FAST FACT NUMBER
*Twelve*

## What Can I Do to Help?

Don't think that there's nothing you can do to help in the fight against AIDS. There are things that all of us can do, from simply telling our friends what we know about AIDS to volunteering at a local AIDS organization.

Some of the things you can do are:

- ask your teacher or principal to invite an AIDS education group to speak at your school. Many AIDS organizations will provide speakers free of charge if you ask them.

- find out who your congresspeople are and write to them, asking that they support funding for AIDS education and research. You can find out who represents you in Congress by asking at your school library.

- volunteer to be a buddy to someone with AIDS or to

help out in some other way at an AIDS organization
or in a hospital with an AIDS unit

• keep informed about AIDS so that you can talk to
your friends and family about it. If you hear someone
saying something negative about people with AIDS
or saying something that isn't correct, educate them.

• write to your local television stations and ask them to
run condom ads or public service announcements
about AIDS. Write to the producers of your favorite
shows and ask them to include safer-sex messages in
their programs. You can usually find addresses for
local television stations in the television guide that
comes in the Sunday paper. You can find out who
produces a television program by watching the cred-
its at the beginning or end of a show. You can write
to these people in care of the television station the
show runs on.

• participate in AIDS walks and other events to raise
money for AIDS organizations, either by participating yourself or by supporting someone else who is
participating

• ask your parents to help you get your school to provide AIDS education if it is not already doing so

*Kate Barnhart*

# ACTING UP TO FIGHT AIDS

*When she was a sophomore in high school, Kate Barnhart joined the AIDS Coalition to Unleash Power (ACT UP), one of the first and most influential AIDS activist groups in the United States, because she felt that AIDS was a problem she wanted to address. She quickly became one of the leaders of ACT UP's Youth Education Life Line (YELL), which focuses on issues of AIDS education as it impacts young people. In her role there she has led protests, organized educational programs that have been used in schools, and has even been arrested for her commitment to speaking out in the fight against AIDS.*

*In addition to her involvement with YELL, Kate, now eighteen, also works in the HIV/AIDS education program of New York City's Coalition of Peer Educators (COPE), where she teaches other young people how to educate themselves*

*and others about HIV and AIDS. She has trav-
eled to AIDS conferences all over the United
States and even abroad to speak out about the
issues facing young people and women with
AIDS. Now in college, she majors in the study of
infectious diseases. A strong voice in the fight
against AIDS, Kate has proved that young people
can make a difference.*

**How did you become involved in AIDS activism?**
I kind of just grew into it, because I grew up in New
York in the early 1980s and I grew up in a community where being gay was the norm. Because the gay
community was one of the hardest hit in the early
years of the crisis, it wasn't like I had to discover that
AIDS was out there. It was always in the background
of my life.

A lot of older people, like neighbors and friends of
my parents, were dealing with it. So it was never a
mystery to me. A lot of kids my age were exposed to
activism at an early age, since our parents were radi-
cals in the 1960s. I wound up at marches and demon-
strations when I was very young. In junior high, the
expectation was that we were going to be social-
justice people as well.

**And you chose to work on AIDS issues?**
Not at first. I worked on human rights issues relating
to El Salvador for a while, and then clean water. Then

the Persian Gulf War came along and I did that, too. They all seemed equally important to me, but none of them were particularly compelling. I hadn't even considered AIDS a political issue because, being around it for so much of my life, it seemed like it was just there, part of the normal way things were.

During the Gulf War, some of us at school had started an organization called Students Against War. Then after the war ended, we wanted to keep the group going, because it was the first politically active network of high school students in New York. We thought it was important to stay together. We had all been some kind of activists before the war. We all had our causes. So we broke SAW into committees based on our interests and renamed ourselves STAND, which was Students Taking Action for a New Direction.

Eventually, STAND and ACT UP ended up doing a demonstration together. Six members of ACT UP and six students of STAND got arrested for taking over the office of a public official as a protest. We were sitting in the police precinct for a long time, and since all twelve of us were chained together, there wasn't much else to do but talk, so we talked about AIDS.

**Did you find that people didn't take you seriously because you were a young person?**
There are two views that former liberals, people from

my parents' generation, take when it comes to young people and activism. The first is where they want you to have their ideas, but then if you take action on them, especially to the point of getting arrested, then suddenly they aren't too happy about it. It's like they don't mind if you recycle, but nothing stronger than that.

The other take is the one held by these revolutionary, heavy-duty groups, which is that they try to recruit you. Like during the Gulf War, these really militant antiwar people were constantly putting young people in arrest situations even though we hadn't been trained or were even aware that we were in potentially dangerous situations. Looking back, I see that they were doing it because we could get arrested and, because of our ages, not have any sort of record of it. So they were using us, and manipulating us. It was really sad.

**How did that affect your decision to join ACT UP?**
When I talked to these people from ACT UP, it was the first time I'd ever met adults who were not trying to manipulate me, who were supportive.

**Is that a big problem for student groups?**
Very much so. It was always a battle to keep student groups student groups and protect them from adult manipulation. There were always adult workers from other activist groups coming to STAND meetings.

And their purpose wasn't to help us or support us, but to colonize us and try to take over.

**Was ACT UP more supportive?**
The day we were arrested, there happened to be an ACT UP meeting that evening. So we went to it and we stood up in front of this whole roomful of people and told them what we had done. And it was such an incredibly supportive group of people, and I felt real-ly comfortable there. I found that in ACT UP people didn't care what my age was. I never felt like people were thinking I was too young or saying, "Oh, she's just a kid."

**What does YELL do?**
YELL is the committee of ACT UP that focuses on adolescent issues in the AIDS crisis. We focus a lot on education, because a lot of the other stuff is damage control. As important as treatment activism is—and finding housing for people with AIDS is really impor-tant—it's damage control. Once people are already infected or already have AIDS, there's a limit to what you can do for them. We want to reach people before they ever have to need those services. So a lot of our focus has been on getting more explicit safer-sex and safer-drug-use information into the hands of people who are young enough that they haven't started engaging in risky behaviors yet. Because if you give people safer-sex information after they start having

sex, not only have they probably already put themselves at risk, but they've also set behavioral patterns. And it's very hard to change behavioral patterns.

**Do you go into schools?**
Well, we try to. ACT UP is considered quite radical, and because of that we don't have as much access to schools as a more conservative group might. And here in New York, even the conservative AIDS education groups are being banned from public schools. A lot of what we do is we hand out information in front of schools. We were handing out condoms a long time before New York had a condom availability program. And now that parents are allowed to say that their children can't be given AIDS information or condoms, we hand out these things at schools to protest that. We also hand out information and condoms at junior high schools, because our whole thing is about getting this information to kids who are young enough that they aren't set in their behavior patterns.

Occasionally, some radical teacher will invite me in to talk to his or her class about AIDS. And then I work on the concept of peer education. I have a program called Youth, AIDS, and Activism that I use, which teaches young people how to organize around AIDS in their school or community. So I tell them how to start a group or what to say if they go to the board of education to try to get an AIDS group estab-

lished in their school. It trains people how to get
involved in the process of activism.

**Is that something more young people are interested
in now?**
Young people see the AIDS crisis more clearly than
adults in many ways. Even most young people who
personally support the idea of complete abstinence
still feel that safer-sex and safer-drug-use information
should be there for those who need it. I have never
met a young person who thought that this information should not be in the schools or that it is disgust-
ing to talk about. It's the adults who say that.

When you explain to young people that keeping
this information out of schools is really all about cen-
sorship, then they become very angry. Young people
tend to have a lot of frustrations about the educational system anyway, so we like to show them how
to channel that frustration into something positive
instead of having them go and chain themselves to
the principal because they don't like their math
teacher or something.

**You've been arrested for some of your work, right?**
I have, but that's not really any big deal. A lot of people think ACT UP just charges out and gets arrested
for the sake of it, and that's a big misconception.
There's a lot that happens before we resort to civil
disobedience. We start off by sending letters to the

people we have a problem with, explaining what our concerns are and asking for a meeting. We ask for a meeting with them and try to negotiate. If they won't respond, then we send a lot of letters or have a lot of people call them. Then we'll try legal forms of demonstrating first. Chaining yourself to a building or doing something illegal is the last resort, because it takes a lot of work.

A lot of people think we do it just for fun, but basically we get arrested for one of two reasons. One is that we break a law that we don't like or feel is unfair. For example, needle exchanges, where you provide IV drug users with clean needles, are illegal in many places. But we feel that is something that is really important, so we will go and hand out needles, which is directly breaking a law we don't agree with. So then you get arrested, but that then gives you the chance to bring a legal challenge against this law that you don't agree with.

The other way, civil disobedience, can be completely symbolic. For example, a couple of years ago a lot of students in the public schools felt that we were being denied a voice by the board of education. So because we felt that they were locking us out of the board, we decided to physically lock them into their office. At five o'clock, when everyone was trying to leave, we chained ourselves across the building. And that was really symbolic. We weren't breaking a law against chaining yourself to a public building because we thought that law was wrong, even though it would make it easier for us if that law was gone. We were doing it to make a point.

The other thing people should know is that we plan these things very carefully. Everyone who participates is supposed to be trained. Plus, we have support people whose job is not to get arrested but to watch the arrests and make sure that everyone who is arrested comes out again okay. We usually have someone with a video camera, and we have lawyers and a completely organized system. And we talk to our lawyers beforehand and find out what the possible consequences are, and we make very informed decisions.

**How important is it that young people get involved in the AIDS crisis?**
I was standing outside the board of education a few months ago demonstrating, and the local Catholic television station, which is always there, came up to interview me. They asked me if I used condoms. When I said I didn't, they got all excited, thinking that they had caught this AIDS education activist in a trap. So the reporter said, "You mean you don't use condoms during sex?" And I told him that I didn't have sex, which made him even more excited because he thought that I was saying that I believed in abstinence, which I wasn't. He said, "Well, since you believe in abstinence, would you recommend that

other young people do as you do?" I looked right at him and said, "Sure, I would recommend that all young people spend their time out here on the streets demonstrating for AIDS education." It was not what he wanted to hear. I think everybody and anybody should do some kind of activist work, whether it's AIDS or something else.

I don't just do AIDS work. I also do youth-liberation work. The truth is that youth in this society have no rights; we are our parents' property.

For me, AIDS is a disease that affects primarily people who are oppressed in some way, whether it be women, poor people, people of color, people without much education, people who are gay, whatever. Youth are just one of those oppressed groups. Everybody always talks about sexism or racism or homophobia, but no one talks about ageism unless it's in the opposite direction, to discuss elderly people being discriminated against. And I sympathize with those people. But at least they can represent themselves in court if they have to. Young people can't. We can go to war and die for our country, but we have very little to say about what kind of information we are allowed to have.

I think young people should be active, if not around AIDS, which I wish they would be, then around youth rights. And AIDS lies within that issue anyway. For instance, if we had the right to uncensored education, then AIDS wouldn't be as much of a problem. Or if we had the right to medical care without parental consent. That is a huge issue for young people, whether they have HIV or not. You go to an emergency room, and they won't do anything until they call your parents. And for many kids, the reason they're bleeding in the first place is because a parent beat them up.

**When it comes to being involved in AIDS, do you think a lot of young people aren't involved because they still think they aren't at risk?**
I think young people don't know how they can get involved. I get letters all the time from young people all over the country asking for help.

**How do you help them?**
First of all, I keep a national database. So anybody who writes to YELL for information, they go into the database. Then, if I get a letter from someone else in the same town or area, I'll hook them up. I've hooked up more pen pals this way, and it really helps to have someone to talk to.

We also send everyone who writes to us safer-sex information, basic AIDS information, and information about YELL and starting their own groups. We just try to do the best we can with each individual letter. It depends on what people need. And we're working on a guide called "How to YELL" so that people can organize in their own areas. It answers questions about things like what to do if your school won't let you meet in the school building, how to fight the board of education if they try to tell you no, that kind of thing. It's so important to educate young people about these things, because until they know, they can't fight for themselves effectively.

**How do you think other people view your work with ACT UP and COPE?**
When I was applying to colleges, I had to write an entrance essay, which was "What was your most positive educational experience?" And of course they were expecting me to describe my favorite biology class or something. And I wrote all about my work with ACT UP. I was rejected by ten schools. But I figured I didn't want to go to any school that wouldn't accept me for who I am anyway.

**Do you get any negative response from older people in the AIDS activism world?**
That varies. For example, in the feminist movement, I think older women really expect the younger women to feel indebted. And that's just not helpful. And then other movements I've been involved in, the older people think the younger ones are really cute for being involved, but they don't put much faith in us.

In AIDS you have a different situation, because many AIDS activists tend to be on the younger side. And that's partly because they die before they have a chance to get very old. And another part of it is that this is a relatively new movement, so there's more flexibility. I think the general feeling in AIDS activism is that we need everybody we can get to fight, so people aren't worried about how old you are or where you come from or what color you are.

**How is your work with COPE different from your work with YELL?**
I call it my dual personality. It's the dichotomy between activism and service. With YELL, we aren't always doing the education ourselves; what we are doing is removing the barriers that prevent other people from doing education. COPE is purely educational.

One of the problems with peer education is that it is usually adults trying to tell young people how to do the job, so you always have this teacher-student relationship. But when you are trying to train peer educators, you should all be peers. With AIDS, we now have so many young people with firsthand expertise in the disease that it's really ridiculous not to draw on that experience. And that's the philosophy behind COPE, that young people teach other young people how to go into their communities and present AIDS information to their peers.

**What kind of young people do you work with in COPE?**

I work with young felons who are in an alternative sentencing program. These are kids who have been convicted of robbery, drug selling, and violent crimes. Instead of spending time in jail, they are given the opportunity to do community service by participating in one of a number of programs. AIDS education is just one of them. So the kids involved in the HIV/AIDS peer educator program all want to be there. Most of them are HIV-affected in some way, either because someone in their family is infected or has died or because a friend is. Sometimes they themselves are infected.

**It must make you very proud to watch them go out and use what you've taught them.**
Oh yeah. Sometimes it's very frustrating, but it's just amazing to see. People have a lot of stereotypes about criminals. I know I did. But they aren't evil people, and this has really shown me how we all have prejudices, even if we aren't aware of them.

It's also great because usually we're the first people their own age who have ever talked to them in straight terms about HIV and AIDS. We go in and we tell them, "Like other young people, we feel that adults have dropped the ball on AIDS education. And we're here to pick it back up again. Because in the end it's up to us to save our own." And then they really listen.

**Is it going to be young people who make the difference in the battle against AIDS?**

Totally. I mean, I'm still fighting the board of ed, but I feel like that is a losing battle. Every time we gain something, we lose it again. And that's because that whole fight is not about AIDS; it's not about young people; it's not about education. It's about politics. That's what's going on with all of this AIDS education in schools.

So what we need is young people to do it for themselves. Because we aren't worried about our political careers. We can just do it. And another part of that is, they can ban ACT UP, they can ban AIDS organizations from schools, they can ban whoever they want. But they can't ban students from school. If young people are educated so that they can tell each other the facts, that cuts right through everything else.

**What is your advice to other young people who might want to get involved?**

I have this diagram that I like to use, and it's very simple. It's a dot surrounded by a circle surrounded by another circle. The dot in the middle is the individual. And that individual has to educate her- or himself. The first circle is family and friends, which means simply telling the people in your life about AIDS. The final circle is the community, which means talking to strangers about AIDS. And that's the final step. It's really that easy. It all starts with educating yourself.

**What's been the most rewarding thing for you about being involved in AIDS activism?**
That's really hard to answer. I can see the people who are infected, and I can see the people who have AIDS, and I can see the people who have died. But I can't see the people who haven't been infected. So to me that's the most frustrating part about it, because you can't see what the results of your work are. It's like I'm fighting for a group of people who I will never know if I won for. The bottom line is, I can't follow people around to watch what they do. I can hand out as many condoms or clean needles as I can get my hands on, but I never know if doing that saved someone's life.

What helps is when I stand up in front of a classroom and explain to people the difference between HIV and AIDS, or draw a diagram to show them what the immune system is. When I see kids who never got the biology before or people who can't read begin to understand for the first time what I'm talking about, that's when it's worth it. When I see things click, when I see people realize that HIV and AIDS are not the same thing, or that people with AIDS die from an indicator disease and not from HIV itself. Especially if you're explaining it to someone who has just tested positive, and you see that relief when they suddenly realize that they're not going to die tomorrow. That really helps. I like that.

And I guess I feel the most positive when I organize a demonstration. There was this one march we did from City Hall across the Brooklyn Bridge to the board of ed offices. And we had enough youth that we really were in the front of the march, leading it. It was just amazing to me to see all of these kids and know that it was something that came from an idea I had one day when I was eating dinner. Or when I do interviews and then people come up to me on the street or send me mail and people mention the article. That tells me that people are listening to what I have to say. Because I could give interviews from now until doomsday, but if nobody reads the stuff, then it doesn't matter.

Also, it helps when adults have these minor revelations and realize that young people can do something. So that's very important to me too.

**Will AIDS education always be part of your life?**
I can't help it. I'll be on my way home tonight on the subway, sitting next to someone, and the odds are I'll be talking to that person about AIDS before they get off. It's just automatic now. In a way, I feel like I'm losing myself in AIDS, because AIDS is so important, and the more you work in this area, the more people you know with HIV and AIDS, and therefore the more people you know who will eventually die. So it

feeds itself. Every person who dies, I feel like I have to take on more of their work.

**Does it make you feel like you've grown up too fast?**
It's had a weird effect on me. I feel like all this time is going by so quickly, but I'm standing still. Sometimes I really don't believe I'll get to be thirty, simply because so many people in the AIDS community don't, and the idea of getting old is just so unreal to me. It's just not something you think of when you see people dying so young all the time.

And it's really changed the people who are my friends. I still have a few friends from what I call my pre-AIDS life, or people I knew when I was only involved a few days a week instead of all the time. But now it's all the time. It's part of me. AIDS doesn't take holidays.

**Do you resent that?**
Sometimes. What I'm angry about now is that I used to be able to sleep and not dream about AIDS. But now it's like I'm dreaming about it three or four nights a week and it never leaves me alone. I have a few non-AIDS friends, but even those people are slowly getting pulled into it. It's like, if you want to be my friend, you have to know about AIDS. I miss me sometimes, but it's just who I am.

There just isn't time to do other stuff. It's like I'll be standing in a line for something and I'll be thinking, "Okay, a person dies from AIDS every seven minutes, and I've been here for fourteen minutes." That's when I wonder if it will ever go away.

But I've also learned so much about myself and about things like death. A lot of young people are very frightened or fascinated by death, but for me it's become very matter-of-fact. I'm not afraid to die now, because I know all of my friends will be waiting for me. And knowing them, they'll probably have some committee for me to be on when I get there.

# For Further Information

If you would like more information about HIV and AIDS, or if you have questions that you need answered, two of the best sources of information are:

**National AIDS Clearinghouse**
The National AIDS Clearinghouse offers printed information on HIV and AIDS free of charge. If your school has an AIDS education program, or wants to start one, you can obtain information on many different issues related to AIDS from the clearinghouse by writing to them at:

National AIDS Clearinghouse
P.O. Box 6003
Rockville, MD 20850

**National AIDS Hotline**
If you have questions about HIV and AIDS, you can

easily get information by calling the National AIDS Hotline. It is operated by the Centers for Disease Control and is the most reliable source of information about HIV and AIDS. The counselors who answer the phone have many resources available to them and can answer questions about HIV and AIDS as well as refer you to organizations in your area that deal with whatever issues you are concerned about. Calls to the hotline are toll free, so you will not be charged for them. The hotline can be reached by calling:

National AIDS Hotline
1-800-342-AIDS
1-800-342-2437
24 hours a day, every day

National AIDS Hotline in Spanish
1-800-344-SIDA
1-800-344-7432
8:00 A.M.–2:00 A.M. every day

National AIDS Hotline for the Hearing Impaired
1-800-243-7889
10:00 A.M.–10:00 P.M. Monday–Friday

In addition to the National AIDS Clearinghouse, there are many local and national AIDS organizations that can provide you with more information about HIV and AIDS. If you are interested in locating AIDS organizations in your area, you can usually find them in the yellow pages by looking under AIDS. If you cannot find any local organizations, try calling your local gay-and-lesbian community center, groups like Planned Parenthood, or health centers, and asking them to recommend some.

If you would like to contact any of the people featured in *The Voices of AIDS* or would like information on the organizations they are part of, you can write to them at the following addresses:

Gabriel Morales and Antigone Hodgins
B.A.Y. Positives
518 Waller
San Francisco, CA 94117

Eileen Mitzman
Mothers' Voices
150 West Twenty-sixth Street
New York, NY 10001

Kyle Craney and Ramona Smith
c/o National Association of People with AIDS
10th Floor
1413 K Street NW
Washington, DC 20005

Dini von Mueffling
Love Heals
345 Park Avenue
New York, NY 10022

Faye Zealand
AIDS Resource Foundation for Children
182 Rosville Avenue
Newark, NJ 07107

Penny Raife Durant
c/o Atheneum Books
866 Third Avenue
New York, NY 10022

Philippa Lawson
HIV Community Coalition
Room 4103
1255 Twenty-third Street NW
Washington, DC 20037

John Carlin
Red Hot Organization
Suite 602
73 Spring Street
New York, NY 10012

Kate Barnhart
ACT UP
135 West Twenty-ninth Street
New York, NY 10001

# Index